The
Bigot

The
Bigot

Why Prejudice Persists

Stephen Eric Bronner

Yale

UNIVERSITY PRESS

NEW HAVEN & LONDON

Yale University Press books may be purchased in quantity for educational,
business, or promotional use. For information, please e-mail
sales.press@yale.edu (US office) or sales@yaleup.co.uk (UK office).

Set in Janson type by Integrated Publishing Solutions.
Printed in the United States of America.

Library of Congress Cataloging-in-Publication Data

Bronner, Stephen Eric, 1949–
The bigot : why prejudice persists / Stephen Eric Bronner.
pages cm
Includes bibliographical references and index.
ISBN 978-0-300-16251-6 (hardback)
1. Prejudices. 2. Toleration. 3. Political science—Philosophy. I. Title.
HM1091.B76 2014
303.3'85–dc23   2013047875

A catalogue record for this book is available from the British Library.

This paper meets the requirements of ANSI/NISO Z39.48–1992
(Permanence of Paper).

10 9 8 7 6 5 4 3 2 1

To my uncle and aunt, Herman and Lore Haller

There is nothing more frightening than ignorance in action.
—*Johann Wolfgang von Goethe*

Hatred alone warms the heart.
—*Umberto Eco*

Contents

Acknowledgments, ix
Introduction, 1

ONE
Modernity, 13

TWO
Mythological Thinking, 54

THREE
Playing the Role, 99

FOUR
The Bigot Today, 154

Appendix: Beginnings, 196
Notes, 201
Index, 223

Acknowledgments

There are many who contributed to this manuscript. My friends Philip Green, Jeffrey Isaac, Edward Ramsamy, and Cornel West offered valuable insights and comments. George Castiglia and Beth Breslaw participated in a seminar devoted to *The Bigot* that was attended by a number of my graduate students: Karie Gubbins, Bill Hwang, Douglas Irvin-Erickson, Edwin Daniel Jacob, Megan Unden, and Sarah Weirich. I would also like to thank my research assistant, Bailey Socha, my manuscript editors, Laura Jones Dooley and Julie Carlson, and especially William Frucht, my editor at Yale University Press, for their help in bringing this work to fruition. Finally, I want to express my gratitude for the ongoing support and enthusiasm shown by my colleagues Alex Hinton and Nela Navarro at Rutgers's Center for the Study of Genocide and Human Rights—as well as by my wife: Anne Burns.

The
Bigot

Introduction

The Bigot was finished a few days after the reelection of President Barack Obama in 2012. I had already begun thinking about a book of this sort shortly after his initial victory in 2008. It was seen by much of the radical right as representing the triumph of multicultural radicalism bolstered by a new vanguard of elite, cosmopolitan urban intellectuals and people of color—all with liberal values and "socialist" hopes. From the moment that Barack Obama entered the White House in 2008, Senate Minority Leader Mitch McConnell (R-Kentucky) stated bluntly that the primary goal of the Republican Party was to block the new administration and ruin any chance that the nation's first black president might have for reelection. Action at the grassroots accompanied this agenda. Fueled by the rhetoric of Fox News and media demagogues like Rush Limbaugh, Glenn Beck, and Michael Savage, and inspired by evangelical fundamentalism, far-right groups routinely began referring to Barack Obama as "the affirmative action president," "the food stamp president," an imam, and the Antichrist. His election would, it was claimed, lead "radical Islamists" to dance in the streets. He was excoriated as an African American (more African than American) who lacked a birth certificate, gained his position illegally, and was complicit in planning the takeover of the United States by the United Nations. Posters and advertisements identified Obama with Hitler, placed his head and that of his wife on the body of chimpanzees, portrayed the White House with rows of watermelons on the lawn, and implied that the president was a crack addict. The problem apparently was not with prejudiced whites who hated blacks but rather with the sophisticated black intellectual who had (always) hated whites. The language of intolerance seemed to have gained a new dialect, one that achieved legitimacy and acceptance among a growing public.

While writing this volume, I often thought of Tyler Clementi, a gay music student at Rutgers University who committed suicide after learning that his roommate had taped his sexual encounter with another man and then spread it across the Internet. Tensions at Rutgers, where I teach, simmer between Muslim students uncritical of their own prejudices and elements of the Jewish community who apparently think that Cossacks are readying themselves for the next pogrom. Intimidated immigrant students huddle together in lunchrooms and cafés. Snickers are audible when a transgender person walks by. Religious intolerance and unease over gay marriage are more common than many might think. Too many young people are skeptical about government policies helpful to a working class—and a working poor—that is no longer white. Even while courses on cultural understanding multiply, and interracial dating has become more acceptable, bigotry flourishes. The university may have its written and unwritten rules of liberal decorum—but academia is not insulated from the outside world.

I didn't write this book with the naive idea of converting bigots. If one or two of them, or their friends, should read it and change their opinions, then so much the better—but I have my doubts. My concern here is also not with analytically defining a philosophical category, specifying an empirical determination, providing inspirational tales of struggles against discrimination or persecution, or condemning an epithet. This book has a different purpose in mind. Like *A Rumor about the Jews* and *Reclaiming the Enlightenment*, it is intended to help educate the bigot's enemies. Classic studies have insightfully analyzed different prejudices such as anti-Semitism, homophobia, racism, sexism, and religious intolerance. In practice, however, it makes little sense to compartmentalize them: the bigot rarely has only one target for his hatred. Prejudices tend to intersect in their ideological and political expressions. Solidarity in combating such *clusters of hatred* requires illuminating what is shared by all yet reducible to none.

Understanding the bigot calls for a phenomenological sketch that explains why prejudice appeals to him, how he chooses his targets, and what impulses are common to his worldview. Quick dabs are necessary to shade his frustrations, brushstrokes highlight his way of thinking about the world, bold lines demarcate the roles that he plays, and touches of color enhance his political ambitions. A phenomenological perspective on the bigot fosters an interdisciplinary investigation that weaves together the existential, psychological, sociological, and political elements shaping what Jean-Paul Sartre once termed "the etiology of hatred."

The Bigot seeks to begin this kind of discussion. Its subject is complex. The bigot is not always white, not always male, not always rich, and not always conservative or fascistic. (To simplify the presentation in this book, however, I have portrayed the bigot as male.) He has joined various political parties and movements. His style changes in different historical circumstances. But there are unifying impulses. The bigot always directs his hatred against those who threaten (or might threaten) his privileges, his existential sense of self-worth, and the (imaginary) world in which he was once at home. In that world, the bigot felt little guilt. His prejudice was the common currency. Few thought there was anything wrong with it. The bigot was comfortable, happy, and even genial. He often engaged in small acts of individual kindness to the subaltern in his own version of noblesse oblige. But his attitude changed once the subaltern no longer accepted his hegemony. The bigot's world then became subject to criticism; it invited comparison with more democratic forms of society. His increasing resentment against those who were turning his world topsy-turvy was a logical consequence.

Sickened by the strivings of the subaltern, and limited by his own cognitive framework, the bigot is a prisoner of his prejudices. He validates himself by employing myths, stereotypes, and double standards. Conspiracy fetishism is always appealing. He is unwilling and unable to engage those who question his opinions or challenge his self-styled superiority. The less he understands the dynamics of modern life, the more insecure he becomes, and the more fanaticism becomes an option. Little wonder then that the bigot should often appear in traditional roles that are associated with an imaginary organic community: the true believer, the elitist, and the chauvinist. These roles are not mutually exclusive and, in fact, usually overlap. The degree of intensity with which they are played varies according to circumstances and the psychological makeup of the individual. But they are all susceptible to fanaticism and they all provide the bigot with a clear conscience. Without this understanding, his role playing makes no sense at all. As a true believer, the bigot hears the Lord's voice and he condemns those who don't, or interpret it otherwise; as the elitist, he knows what's what and thereby insists on his superiority to those of other races, ethnicities, and gender orientations with different views; and, in the role of the chauvinist, his attitudes are the authentic expression of his community.

None of these roles is identical with intolerance or prejudice. There are gentle, tolerant, and progressive believers in every faith; elitists are not always bigots or even reactionaries; and chauvinists are often genuine champions of tradition and community. Each role can take a variety of forms: the true believer need not be a member of a church, the elitist can be a populist, and the chauvinist can be a loner. But they all serve the bigot well when fueled by contempt, intolerance, paranoia, and a desire for revenge. These roles justify his attempts to limit participation in what is (obviously) *his* world. Each helps identify the exploited and marginalized subaltern with the unalterable evil, inferior, and alien traits of the Other.

The word *prejudice* derives from the Latin *praejudicum:* a judgment made in advance of a trial. Its appeal is readily apparent. Prejudice makes every judgment simple and insulates it from criticism or reflection. The bigot's moral cognition and his intellectual outlook are constituted within a parochial life-world that is neither accountable nor transparent. He hides behind its traditions and established habits. But conformity is not much of an excuse. There have always been people who rebelled against the prejudices of their society and who refused to become bigots. There is always an ineradicable element of individual responsibility in prejudice that the bigot himself is unwilling to admit and anxious to obscure. That makes him content with how old beliefs, old rumors, and old loyalties congeal into myths and, in turn, beget stereotypes that justify his use of the double standard. The bigot's prejudices rest on pre-reflective assumptions that become fixed, finished, and irreversible in the face of new knowledge, and thus shut down discourse.[1]

Almost by definition, the bigot's prejudice is hostile, destructive, and malignant. It crystallizes myriad forces that are learned (consciously or unconsciously) and then internalized. More is involved here than an individual with his particular psychological problems. As an anti-Semite, the bigot might exhibit an obsessive personality; as a sexist, he could be a narcissist; as a racist, he might harbor sexual fears or castration anxieties.[2] Each bigot has his own neuroses, family conflicts, relatives, friends, social circles, geographical settings, and privileged targets of hatred. He is most often a member of the lower middle class, a small shop owner, or a farmer—though industrial workers and others can also prove racist and authoritarian in orientation. Not every social group or stratum will exhibit every prejudice: the bigot in one group is often the target of prejudice by bigots in other groups. But the bigot's goal is always the same: to transform a living, disenfranchised, exploited, and persecuted subaltern into an object for his use, an Other whose fixed traits render him unholy, unnatural, or inferior.

For all the bluster, the bigot's ego is extremely fragile.[3] Perhaps that explains why he is happiest in a fascist or authoritarian regime. But he can also survive in a representative democracy and even under local participatory forms of rule. He is willing to join any movement: conservative, fascist, liberal, socialist, or communist. Again and again, however, he plays similar reactionary roles in public life. Language often fails him. Studies suggest that behind his words are "numerous, reified, stereotypical ideas and formulations whose very form implies that they do not reflect speakers' opinions but, instead, are spoken without conscious intent."[4] The bigot's frustration is understandable. Intellectuals, experts, politicians, and other outsiders seemingly have no respect for the bigot's opinions and traditions. The atheist, the foreigner, the homosexual, and the other subversives are all seeking to change the natural order of things. The open society threatens the bigot's hegemony and thus he engages in a politics that seeks to narrow the public sphere. Participation should be limited to those who are like him. Those unlike him are only conspiring against him anyway. They might be those who killed Christ, brought about the last economic crash, engaged in cultural subversion, blasphemed against Allah, exhibited ingratitude for the benefits that civilization has bestowed—or caused 9/11 either by supporting the attacks or by bringing God's wrath down on America. It doesn't really matter.

Once the beneficiary of social privilege, the bigot now views himself as a loser—or as a winner under siege. Imaginary events are used to indict entire races, religions, nationalities, or gender groups. The bigot's need for excuses is unending: it is always about him and never about his victims. What the subaltern endured is irrelevant. It's time to "move on" and "get over it." The bigot has heard enough whining about gringos, slavery, the Holocaust, and the rest. And, besides, there are always two sides to the story: Santa Anna was no democrat; Southern slaves supposedly had it better than Northern workers; some Jews were killed, but then Germans also died in the Allied bombings. Explanations become excuses; qualifications build on one another; at the end of the day, the sufferings of the subaltern blend into the vicissitudes of a broader tradition that the bigot feels he represents. His people too have suffered—undoubtedly more than any other group. The bigot twists history, obscures the need for ethical responsibility, and seeks to eradicate the difference between victim and persecutor. Fabricated relativism provides the bigot with his "pseudo-orientation in an estranged society."[5] It gives him a veneer of tolerance and it justifies his parochial indifference to the plight of the subaltern and other cultures, and what might be learned from them.

The bigot is a relativist but not a pluralist. The distinction is important. Both pluralism and relativism may militate against the idea that any single truth will show us the way to paradise. But pluralism assumes liberal institutions and universal ideals: it allows individuals to make reasoned judgments about other cultures and it is accepting of different lifestyles.[6] None of this interests the bigot. He has as little use for notions of reciprocity as he does for conversations about the falsifiable character of truth claims. His only real concern is with maintaining his superiority and finding a creative alibi for his failings.

No wonder that the bigot suffers from an identity deficit. Every encounter with the Other must therefore confirm his pre-reflective prejudices and superiority. Circumstances dictate whether he advocates legality or illegality, violence or persuasion, reform or revolution. The bigot is a partisan who does not privilege any particular form of party organization.[7] He will sometimes mouth nationalist slogans and at other times proclaim his international solidarity with the white race. Sometimes he will support the welfare state, sometimes not. The bigot can appear as an elitist, arrogantly condemning the mob, or as a populist raging against urban liberals, international bankers, and outsiders. Or, like the Klansman and the Nazi, he can appear as an elitist and a populist simultaneously. The bigot can shift his views so easily because, ultimately, he has no views—only interests and prejudices that are mutually reinforcing. Bigotry is thus not "properly speaking a social theory, which integrates various elements into a global and coherent vision of society and history. It . . . distorts social theories. It draws from a storehouse of components, retaining one or rejecting another according to the ideological needs of the moment."[8]

The bigot's political tactics have changed and his inflammatory rhetoric is no longer quite what it was. His goose step has been shelved. The cult based around a single leader is missing, and the bigot's longing for regime change is mostly under wraps. But the bigot is a resilient creature. He knows how to dissemble. The bigot is not merely identifiable with certain attitudes or psychological traits, or a certain language of intolerance. Words wound but policies wound even more. Prejudice is not confined by what people feel or say but what they actually do. It has an economic as well as a cultural and political dimension. That is especially true today given the opportunities for camouflage provided the bigot by the mass media and political establishment as well as the rise of the Tea Party. His opponents thus require new forms of struggle that highlight not simply solidarity but also a sharper form of political judgment. Even with the best policies and the best will, however, there is no guarantee of final victory. There is no simple solution to the problems posed by the bigot—and this book does not pretend to provide one. Nevertheless, it might just offer some insights about the workings of prejudice and practical approaches for developing an antidote, if not a final cure.

ONE

Modernity

Karl Marx once quipped that "violence is the midwife of every old society pregnant with a new one."[1] Just as surely, however, prejudice is the midwife of violence. The bigot embraced this view from the start. Hatred of the Jews goes back to Egypt and Babylonia. Contempt for what the Greeks considered the "barbarian"—whoever was not of Greece—existed even at the height of the classical period. And Homer already understood the struggles of the outcast and the stranger. What today might be termed ethnic or racial conflicts between empires, religions, tribes, and clans have always shaped the historical landscape.

But there is a sense in which modernity created the bigot. Prior to the democratic revolutions of the eighteenth century, perfectly decent people simply accepted prevailing prejudices as a matter of course. They suffered no opprobrium. Even in early twentieth-century America, few people (other than the targets of prejudice) were especially bothered that major-league baseball admitted only whites, that the armed forces were segregated, that rape and incest were barely mentioned, and that the white male was the standard by which intelligence was judged. The bigot of today, in recalling the jokes and everyday humiliations that these groups endured, seeks to re-create the normality of prejudice. That subaltern groups have proven so successful in resisting his project only intensifies his frustration.

Modernity, with its roots in the European Enlightenment and the democratic revolutions that extended from 1688 to 1789, runs counter to the institutions and beliefs that the bigot holds dear. Its new capitalist production process substitutes exploitation for his hatred. It has little use for established prejudices, revealed truths, or sacred traditions. And its commitment to principles like the liberal rule of law and toleration, republican institutions, and universal rights would inspire attempts by women, people of color, religious minorities, and gays to constrict the arbitrary exercise of authority by church and state.

Modernity liberated the powers of humanity; it generated the idea that people could shape their own fates. This is very different from the bigot's assumption that biology or anatomy is destiny. Modernity relies on the growth of science, technology, and instrumental rationality. What was once taken on faith is now subject to criticism and what was once shrouded in myth and darkness now potentially becomes open to light. The urban and secular character of modernity, its fostering of pluralism and individualism, further militate against the bigot's sensibility. He detests the modern notion of progress that is so intimately connected with what Max Weber termed "the disenchantment of the world."

But the bigot deals with modernity as best he can, for example, by using the same scientific methods as his critics. Architects of the Nazi genocide used mathematical rationality and scientific techniques not merely to keep meticulous records of the prisoners sent to Auschwitz, or to construct the crematoria, but also to reduce corpses to their parts and to use them to create soap, cloth, and fertilizer. But Nazi science was ultimately used to legitimate irrational and unscientific claims. To engage in their genocide, the Nazis needed to assume that their victims were less than human and, in this vein, Kenan Malik was correct in noting that to suggest the infamous "final solution" was a product of "reason" is to "elevate the prejudices of the Third Reich to the status of scientific knowledge."[2]

That being said, the bigot has never felt entirely comfortable in employing science to support his prejudices.

For example, although Mussolini and Hitler may have employed scientists who used the same physics and chemistry for producing military weapons as their counterparts elsewhere, in public, the dictators insisted on the existence of "Italian mathematics" and (in opposition to Einstein and his Jewish colleagues) "German physics." The bigot dislikes universal concepts and objective criteria for making scientific judgments. He prefers giving his prejudices a scientific gloss by making reference to phrenology or by insisting on the primary importance of certain physical attributes, inherited traits, eugenics, and anthropological hierarchies. Genetics has a particular attraction for the bigot seeking to explain intelligence or creativity—though no evidence exists to justify any causal connection between biology and social accomplishment.[3]

The bigot has always felt queasy about transforming the invisible into the visible, the ineffable into the discursive, and the unknown into the known. Observation and evidence, hypothesis and inference, confirmation and validation are thus selectively employed by him to justify what Cornel West has termed "the discursive exclusion" of those who are different and what they have to offer.[4] Science requires an open society, and a liberal culture that allows the questioning of authority.[5] But the bigot has no use for what the young Marx called "the ruthless critique of everything existing."[6] He is always primarily concerned with proving what he already thinks he knows. He insists that the answers to the problems of life have been given and he resents everything that challenges inherited wisdom, parochial prejudices, and what he considers the natural order of things. Thus he is uncertain what to make of capitalism.

Not so deep in his heart, the bigot is an opportunist. Other than his prejudices, he has no core beliefs. The bigot likes it when his interests are being served, when people of color are exploited, but he dislikes it when he feels disadvantaged. In principle he endorses inequality and the idea of competition. But only when he is on top or, better, believes he is on top. The problem arises when he finds himself on the bottom. Competition is good when it works *for him*. When it doesn't, the bigot will insist that his competitors are cheating—and that they cheat because it is a trait of their ethnicity, nationality, or race. Jews conspire against him in ruling Wall Street, immigrants take away his jobs, affirmative action undermines his prospects, and unions and welfare programs have made his country soft.

Caught between fear of capitalists and contempt for workers, admiration for competition and principled dislike of socialism, the bigot vacillates. He imagines how family, neighborhood, and religious ties, in ostracizing the subaltern, have provided the infrastructure of a productive small-town community. He cannot grasp why the bourgeoisie would strip away the "sentimental veil" of the family and the ties that bind men to their "natural superiors." He is aghast at how religious ecstasy can be drowned in the "icy waters of egotistical calculation," a process that leaves no other nexus than "naked self interest" and "cash payment." The bigot is both amazed and repelled by the cultural and material revolutions that have broken down "Chinese walls of tradition" so that "all that is solid melts into air. All that is sacred becomes profane, and man is at last compelled to face with sober senses his real conditions."[7]

The logic of capitalist accumulation baffles the bigot. He cannot comprehend how wealth is ever more surely concentrated in great corporate firms and the class divisions that are generated. He is unable to see that workers are dependent on capital because employment is dependent on investment. He also never draws implications from the fact that profit (not prejudice) spurs capitalist development. Today there are banks geared toward women's interests, a black bourgeoisie, a gay consumer culture, and support among many firms for looser immigration policies. Jews, women, blacks, gays, immigrants, and members of other previously excluded groups have expanded the market and provided a pool of talent that can be fruitfully exploited. But solidarity among working people of different races, genders, and ethnicities is precisely what the bigot rejects. As a consequence, his prejudices serve as a drag on the system even while they fragment opposition to it. Thus he finds himself critical of capital and its liberal impulses but also (perhaps even more) critical of those socialists who contest its power.

Nowhere is this counter-revolutionary undertaking analyzed more trenchantly than in the historical works of Marx and Engels.[8] Rarely noted is that in those works, for the first time, a general theory of the counter-revolution was articulated. Old symbols and myths are repackaged to confront the two dominant forms of thought associated with the two dominant classes that emerged with the modern production process: the liberalism of the revolutionary bourgeoisie and the socialism of an incipient industrial working class. According to this logic, precapitalist values and ideologies should appeal most to precapitalist classes like the aristocracy (or aristocratic pretenders), the petty bourgeoisie (or, in German, the *Mittelstand*), the peasantry, and even the notorious semi-criminal underclass (*Lumpenproletariat*), who are rooted in a community bolstered by religious and traditional values. And that is, indeed, the case. These classes historically served as the mass base for the Ku Klux Klan, European fascism, and modern fundamentalism. Liberals and socialists—albeit usually with a guilty conscience—have also endorsed various imperialist and chauvinist forms of bigotry. Nevertheless, it is what John Dewey termed a "warranted assumption" to suggest that a special affinity has existed between right-wing movements and the bigot: it is not true in every instance but it is true in the vast majority of instances, and it is certainly true today.

These classes vacillate between big business and the working class. Subordinate to the one, they feel superior to the other. They legitimate themselves by embracing "property, family, religion, order" and claiming that they wish to "save" society from "the enemies of society." But they usually forget to mention that just as frequently it is "the circle of its rulers' contracts" that is saved, "as a more exclusive interest is maintained against a wider one. Every demand of the simplest bourgeois financial reform, of the most ordinary liberalism, of the most formal republicanism, the most shallow democracy, is simultaneously castigated as an 'attempt on society' and stigmatized as 'socialism.'"[9] The right-wing agenda links the attack on liberalism and socialism. Its supporters intend to constrict pluralism, civil liberties, economic equality, and (literally) disenfranchise the subaltern. The assault on the "socialist" welfare state is thereby coupled with the attack on "liberal" concerns regarding gays, immigrants, people of color, and women. Supporters of these causes may publicly (and even privately) deny that they are bigots. Nevertheless, they obviously hope to derive power and benefits from policies that foster prejudice.

Prejudice seems to flourish among those groups most marginal to the capitalist accumulation process. The bigot is most often found in nonurban settings and parochial communities among the lower middle class, low-level bureaucrats, small business owners, individual contractors, and farmers—though industrial workers, particularly white men, are among others who can also prove racist and authoritarian.[10] Were such members of such imperiled classes and groups to embrace liberalism or social democracy, or fully identify with capital or labor, it would mean embracing ideologies and classes that view them as anachronisms, their beliefs as standing in the way of progress, and their parochial way of life as irrevocably doomed.[11]

The bigot lags behind the rapid changes generated by capitalism and so is condemned to resist new forms of social and political life.[12] He looks for what is rock solid, what is seemingly beyond circumstance, and he finds his trinity: religion, convention, community. Fierce resentment of modernity's advocates and beneficiaries—cosmopolitans, intellectuals, scientists, and secularists—becomes an intrinsic part of his outlook. This resentment stems not merely from (unconscious) envy of the elite, which was the famous argument of Nietzsche and Max Scheler.[13] It also emanates from the bigot's fear that the forces of modernity are destroying his social privileges, his feeling of self-worth, and his world. He is intent on not only resisting them but also reaffirming and taking back what is his, that which he feels has been unjustly taken from him. The bigot has already heard too much about the injustices that he perpetrated in the past. He is uninterested in dialogue with educated outsiders representing the subaltern who know nothing about his community and who are unwilling to take his views seriously. A right-wing poster makes the bigot's point perfectly: "It doesn't matter what this sign says, you'll call it racism anyway!"

But then it is not simply what the bigot says but also how he says it: the obsessive-compulsive, often even pathological, style in which he organizes his experiences, articulates his words, and expresses his emotions.[14] His style is not a derivative matter but instead a part of his character. The bigot senses that modernity is undermining his belief system and his ability to make sense of himself. This is the source of his identity deficit and what Sartre once described as an "objective neurosis" that projects the causes of his failings on the victim of his prejudice. The success of the subaltern in changing her status leaves the bigot with someone to blame for the demise of his world. The bigot is engaged not only in demeaning the target of his prejudice but also in turning himself into a victim. In his eyes, the real victim becomes the imaginary oppressor and the real oppressor becomes the imaginary victim. The bigot thus feels himself persecuted and his response is often tinged by hysteria. His neurotic style is a form of adaptation. Whether it is fostered by conscious instrumental desires to rationalize behavior, or unconscious desires to deflect guilt, depends on the circumstances.[15] Either way, this style works to confirm the mixture of pessimism and resentment that predominates among those who believe they are losers in the march of progress.

The bigot justifies his entitlement by birth or by inherited privileges sanctified by tradition such as gender, skin color, ethnicity, or lineage. His superiority has nothing to do with work: it has not been earned. The famous line from Pierre Beaumarchais's *The Marriage of Figaro* (1784), which was delivered by a simple barber to his aristocratic nemesis, still packs a punch: "Other than being born what have you ever done to deserve your privileges?"

The bigot can only answer by referring to God's will, innate traits, or tradition.[16] He is content to claim that his privileges are deserved because they have always existed, and that the subaltern is thereby eternally condemned to his inferior status. This view pits the bigot against the most basic contention of modernity and the general political position of the subaltern, namely that social practices are mutable. This helps explain why the subaltern has tended to embrace liberal and socialist ideologies. Part of the struggle for equality fought by Jews, people of color, sexual outsiders, intellectuals, and strangers involves a philosophical attack on fixed assumptions about human nature and on frozen social hierarchies.

As many forms of prejudice are available as there are identities. The bigot simply picks one and insists on the superiority of its (authentic, affirming, and self-serving) narrative to the exclusion of other narratives, its (authentic, affirming, and self-serving) customs to the exclusion of other customs, its (authentic, affirming, and self-serving) feeling of belonging to the exclusion of the Other. By heightening the binary opposition between "us" and "them," the paranoid personality gains an elemental sense of superiority. But that division is then refracted by the bigot in different ways to different groups. The bigot thus embraces cosmopolitanism in reverse: instead of feeling at home everywhere, which Kant considered the essence of cosmopolitanism, he is intent on making perceived outsiders not at home in his community, his nation, his house of worship, or his tribe.[17] The bigot's world is small. There is nothing to learn, little sense of adventure, and less of possibility.

Emerging trends might expand the possibilities for autonomy, tolerance, self-expression, and self-definition.[18]

Human rights have been acknowledged in principle even by nations that have abused them in practice. The bigot, a reactionary by inclination and interest, senses the threat posed by progress—liberal education, toleration, and what I once termed the cosmopolitan sensibility.[19] Progress inveighs against lynchings, pogroms, slavery, and witch trials. It fosters the idea of a common humanity beyond inherited traits, religious differences, and national boundaries. Progress makes it possible for the individual to look outside himself and take into account the longings of the weakest, "the lowly and the insulted."

Mitigating suffering is an imperative that exists within every religion: Jewish law condemns the torture of animals; the Buddha spoke of "selflessness"; Confucius saw himself as part of the human race; Hinduism lauds the journey of life; and Jesus identified with the "lowly and the insulted" in his Sermon on the Mount. What Norbert Elias once termed the "civilizing process" describes the development of compassion, empathy, and toleration not simply for those like us but for those who are different. All of this rubs the bigot against the grain. So far as he is concerned, modernity has brought him nothing but grief. The lyrics to a song played by the white supremacist band Definite Hate sum up his feelings nicely: "What has happened to America/That was once so white and free?"

The Other

As modernity unfolds, the bigot's enemies multiply and he is forced to defend himself on many fronts simultaneously. Powerful conspiracies, revisionist histories, rumblings of discontent from below, and cultural threats to his community swirl around him. Every new criticism, every new demand for equality, every new scientific discovery fills his heart with dismay. Making sense of them all is a herculean task: better to treat them as different expressions of the same impulse. Nazi racial "science" explored not merely the innate traits of Jews but also those of other groups ranging from "Aryans" to the Slavs and the Chinese. The Ku Klux Klan and the Aryan Nation never hated just blacks and Jews; their disgust extended to Catholics and other minorities as well. Because prejudice comes in clusters and its victims are arbitrarily defined, the bigot can place primacy on a particular target as circumstances dictate. He can champion the fight against homosexuality in one situation, religious heretics in another, or Roma in still another. Each target of hatred reinforces the others as an overriding worldview emerges built on stereotypical images. Nowhere is this tendency demonstrated better than when a bigoted fictional character insists the Jew is "as vain as a Spaniard, ignorant as a Croat, greedy as a Levantine, ungrateful as a Maltese, insolent as a Gypsy, dirty as an Englishman, unctuous as a Kalmyk, imperious as a Prussian and as anyone from Asti."[20]

For the bigot, subaltern groups congeal into a single all-encompassing and overwhelming threat. Fighting them calls for narrowing their opportunities, refusing to see them for what they are, and identifying them as inherently inferior with fixed traits and an unchangeable status. Thus the bigot constructs the Other—even as a network of stereotypical images constructs him. That the bigot lacks knowledge about those suffering prejudice serves his purpose. Fantasies about malevolent Arab sheiks, rich Jews controlling London, and shiftless people of color only reinforce this ignorance. Such images are fixed and finished. The bigot fears the prospect of individuals choosing their identities and is unsettled by what they are willing to accept (or deny) with respect to their religions, conventions, and communities. With each such choice, the bigot's standing erodes a little more, and the Other, in expressing his will, threatens to become a subject in his own right.

That is precisely what the bigot wishes to prevent. So he longs for a time when the Other was treated as such: when he was expected to step off the sidewalk as the bigot passed, when the Other never sat on the same bench and didn't drink from the same fountain. Vienna in 1938 had benches with signs stating that Jews and dogs were not permitted to sit on them; Hitler closed public swimming pools to Jews. Imperialist settlers had the same mindset when it came to the colonized peoples. But there was a sense in which the Other remained anonymous: he was everyone in a given group and "no one" in particular. The subaltern vanishes as a living, singular individual. Consequently, she always totters on the edge of becoming one of "them" who threatens the bigot—and "us."[21]

Referring to them and how "they" behave enables the bigot to avoid dealing with any evidence that reflects their real activities. He is uninterested in distinctions. Differences between Islam as a faith and Islam as a political enterprise, or between Sunnis and Shiites, fall by the wayside. Judaism and Zionism become interchangeable. Blacks, gays, Latinos, and women are fashioned into images of what the bigot imagines them to be. This construction is always (whether consciously or unconsciously) designed to serve his interest. Only by imposing anonymity upon the Other can the bigot affirm his own subjectivity. The implications of that dynamic are concrete. The vision of "them" shapes who "we" are: the Other invades our sentiments, our analytic perspectives, and thus our everyday lives. Umberto Eco was correct when he noted that the motto of the bigot is "*Odi ergo sum.* I hate therefore I am."[22]

The bigot requires recognition by the Other to affirm his superiority and his existential sense of self. But he is made uneasy by the mass media and the Internet. He senses his victim's discontent with his lack of freedom, his paralyzed subaltern status, and things as they are. Most of all, however, he intuits the Other's lack of respect for who he, the bigot, is and what he believes. Just as modernity steadily undermines the identification of the subaltern as Other, it also intensifies the bigot's prejudices. His hatred of modernity is thus a function of modernity itself. Fundamentalism, for example, is a modern phenomenon. The quest for purity is a response to the seeming triumph of the profane. In the fundamentalists' view, revenge should be taken against blasphemers and the heretics. But there are so many of them! Old-time religion, family values, and small-town traditions are nearly powerless against global developments predicated upon diversity. The terms of engagement have been set: the bigot is condemned to fight a guerrilla war against the encroachments of the Other and the erosion of his way of life.

This brave new world, for the bigot, generates only confusion and anger. There are now nearly two hundred countries; an explosion in the number of belief systems has taken place; and more than three quarters of the people on the planet speak more than one language. Religions are ever less geographically determined. The Grand Mosque in the holy city of Mecca is now dwarfed by a mammoth clock tower, an imitation of Big Ben, which serves as the centerpiece of a huge shopping mall with an eight-hundred-room luxury hotel. Religious devotion now increasingly occurs in a secular context in which past affiliations are on the decline. There are worship sites on television and on the Internet. Evangelical Christians now pray in "mega-churches" with their own malls and sports complexes or in smaller "gatherings" and spiritual "communities" within their cafes and art galleries; mullahs use cell phones; creationists justify themselves with "research"; and the faithful organize through the web. Religious decisions are increasingly affected by the modern problems of everyday life attendant upon abortion, sex education, homosexuality, and the misconduct of priests. Identity is becoming ever more fluid and susceptible to the world of commodities.

With the emergence of this disenchanted multicultural world, bereft of absolutes and chaotic in the multiplication of possibilities for self-definition, the bigot experiences an identity deficit. The lack of respect he receives only heightens his nostalgia for privileges enjoyed in times past and the traditions that justified them. Little thought is wasted on the Other who suffered the costs. The bigot chose not to look then, and he chooses not to look now. Like Bertolt Brecht's character J. Pierpont Morgan in *Saint Joan of the Stockyards* (1932), who owns a slaughterhouse but cannot look at blood, the bigot turns away from the world that his prejudices helped shape. Most Israelis have not visited the Occupied Territories, few memorials recall the numerous slave revolts in the Americas, Hindus in India consider the Muslims in their midst a "pampered minority," and apologies to the victims of Western imperialism have not exactly been forthcoming.

The bigot is content to cloak the past in sentimentality: the happy slaves in the fields, the happy women in the kitchen, the happy white people with their picket fences, the happy Jews in the ghetto, the happy colonized happily learning the rudiments of civilization from the colonizer. For some reason, however, the subaltern always seems ungrateful. That is intolerable to the bigot. Doubts are thereby created that he cannot bear. They heighten his insecurity, his unconscious guilt, and thus the brutality he employs to expunge those feelings.[23] So far as the bigot is concerned, he is acting in the subaltern's interests—and, even if he isn't, the unjust treatment is only natural and morally necessary.

Living in a world of prefabricated images and stereotypes, the bigot simply cannot understand why the Other should resent him. The only explanation is that the worthless wretch is being fed lies by some alien force: carpetbaggers, intellectuals, communists, or terrorists. The bigot suffers what from what Henri Parens has called "stranger anxiety."[24] The degree to which the bigot is affected by this neurosis is the degree to which his paranoia intensifies. The Other becomes increasingly diffuse and ill-defined, yet increasingly omnipresent. The bigot tends to project his own fear of the Other into rationalizations for why she cannot or will not assimilate. There is always some imputed quality that makes it impossible for her to do so. Jews are too pushy and won't embrace the Savior; gays are depraved and won't engage in "therapy" to "cure" their sexual inclinations; women lack rationality; blacks are lazy and dangerously hypersexualized. All of them consider the bigot their enemy and, so far as he is concerned, their common hatred can only derive from the common resentment of his superiority.

Whatever the controversy, therefore, it is always the aggrieved, never the bigot, who should show restraint. The onus of social responsibility is always on those responding to his provocation. This leads the bigot to adapt his prejudices to meet new conditions. Anti-immigrant sentiments and stereotypes have gracefully shifted from one group to another over time. The supposed laziness of blacks, once considered biological, is now thought to be due to their reliance on the welfare state. Women are no longer unfit for various jobs because of their supposed physical handicaps, but because of their perceived emotional makeup and the pressure of surrendering their traditional roles as homemakers. Under cover of a belief in the Second Coming of Christ, Christian true believers who were once rabidly anti-Semitic have now apparently decided that the next Antichrist will not be a Jew but rather an Arab and that support for Israel is less noxious than the thought of Islam controlling Jerusalem. Nevertheless, the original intent of the bigot remains what it was: the leopard doesn't change its spots.

Whether the bigot has disfigured "the face of the other," in Emmanuel Levinas's phrase, is immaterial. He always feels himself the insulted party: it is his critics who are intolerant and insensitive. The bigot must therefore find ways to justify his aggrieved status—and protect his privileges. So it is that "they" are ruining the neighborhood; "they" are taking advantage of liberal programs and wasting the bigot's tax dollars; "they" are always the culprit. And, since they are the culprit, it makes no sense to let them utilize their civic rights to question the bigot's rectitude and further destroy the community. As he sees it, freedom should belong only to him. The bigot can pray where he wishes and say what he wants. But the freedom that applies to him does not apply to the Other. This double standard is a necessary consequence of bigotry— and it always has political ramifications. It has become a common refrain, in complaining about the spread of Islam in the West, to suggest that building a mosque is different from building a synagogue because the former constitutes a political statement or provocation. Similar sentiments informed the bitter controversy over whether a mosque might be constructed in New York City at "Ground Zero."

The language of intolerance seems eminently reasonable to the bigot. Manichean assumptions define his world: he is unconcerned with nuance. That is why, today, gays make such a convenient target. Their practices are deemed unnatural or self-consciously perverse. Being gay is either an unalterable biological determination that makes the gay person appear abnormal, or it is a choice that thereby renders him purposefully degenerate. Either way, the gay person challenges what it means to be a "real" man or a "real" woman. Gender roles must remain what they were because what they were is "natural"—and what they are now is not. The bigot takes his arguments where he can find them. He is a bricoleur who uses whatever he happens to find along the way. Any text can be made to say anything and the more sacred the better: Old Testament, New Testament, or Koran can all be used to argue that heretics and nonbelievers deserve the sword, women are inferior, homosexuality is a sin, and segregation is natural. If the bigot's critics use the same texts against him, which has happened more than once, then—obviously—they have misread them.

The language of intolerance is unconcerned with argumentation or substantiation. Yet the bigot does not exactly lie: something other than simple falsehood is at work. Lies are subject to falsification, but the bigot's existential self-definition is not. This is the underpinning for the language that he employs to make sense of reality. It short-circuits contradiction. The notion of "deracination," for example, has a self-evident moral connotation for the bigot. But it assumes a notion of race that is elastic in that it can apply to a species, a group with common physical attributes, a nation or ethnicity, or individuals supposedly defined by genetic or genealogical traits.

Today, perhaps, racial categories are more hinted at than employed in public discourse. But they still provide the more intellectually inclined bigot with a point of reference for justifying his superiority and his target's inferiority as well as explaining the decline of society. Intolerance can affect even established philosophical categories like "rootedness," "identity," or "authenticity," when these terms are employed to deny reciprocity and to privilege one particular group over others. Everything is "rooted" in the bigot's "authentic" experience of "identity" so that the categories are hijacked to further the same purpose: invalidate any meaningful standard of responsibility for judging either the bigot or his victim.

During the eighteenth century, calls for tolerance inspired the struggle for a republican state under the liberal rule of law. Free speech was considered the precondition for all other civil liberties: it would have defeated the purpose to insulate this or that religion or this or that religious figure from criticism or even "blasphemy." The extent to which freedom of speech is inhibited was seen as the extent to which pluralism is constrained and the recognition of those who think differently was viewed as an implicit attack on the bigot. In the media age when anyone can say anything and the need for pluralism becomes the justification, however, some maintain that the original understanding of tolerance requires revision. According to them we must now confront the phenomenon of "repressive tolerance" whose proponents believe that the content of speech is always secondary to the right to speak.[25] Their logic permits intolerance, places stupidity on the same level as intelligence, and attempts to bind future generations to the ignorant prejudices of those that preceded them. Repressive tolerance is willing to accept hate speech, flat-out racism, the denial of global warming, or the rejection of evolution as mere matters of opinion.

Every teacher knows that there is no place for hate speech or name-calling in a classroom: it is impolite, intimidating, and disastrous for a meaningful discourse. Challenging intolerance is a difficult cultural and political process in which it is impossible to extrapolate from one society to another. But the common aim is surely securing the possibility of dialogue. A democratic society is based on respect for civil liberties and a willingness to hear what many believe should not be spoken. Dealing with this situation requires common sense mixed with a commitment to tolerance. Those wishing to censor the bigot should remain wary of turning him into a martyr. The defense of free speech should not preclude moral protests against attempts to manipulate tolerance for repressive ends. But moral protests are not the same thing as legislation. To move from one to the other is to play into the bigot's hands. He always tends to favor authority over liberty. Because his aim is to deprive the subaltern of agency, legal censorship is a dangerous way for libertarians to respond and it is even more dangerous to treat its employment as a cause for celebration. There is nothing that the bigot fears more than open dialogue, cosmopolitan sentiments, and pluralism. He knows that these are the cultural trends he must resist if the Other is to remain the Other.

Identity Deficits

Jean-Paul Sartre once said of the anti-Semite that he "turns himself into stone." The bigot flees from his own freedom. Prejudice locks him as well as its target into preestablished categories: neither can alter his fate. The bigot is unwilling to entertain new possibilities, unwilling to think in anything other than stereotypes, and unwilling to change.

He embraces "bad faith" and thus he is inauthentic by definition. In this same vein, according to Sartre, the authentic Jew exhibits good faith only if he recognizes the socially constructed "situation" in which the bigot sees him. Individual freedom is meaningful only in its exercise: the subject has an identity. Only the Jew can confront the anti-Semite with the empirical reality that prejudice ignores. The Jew can have humanist, liberal, and socialist supporters. No one else, however, can challenge the anti-Semite in quite the same way.

Sartre's *Anti-Semite and Jew* caused a sensation when it first appeared in 1947. But its implications have often been misunderstood and its salience narrowed. Sartre's approach is relevant for understanding not just the anti-Semite but the bigot in general. His view of identity, with its emphasis on the conscious exercise of freedom, describes a basic influence on struggles undertaken by other targets of prejudice. The bigot no less than his victim experiences the existential impulse toward self-definition: ethics becomes a function of whether the individual is willing to take responsibility for this impulse and how it is translated into action in the given "situation."

With its emphasis on individual freedom and personal responsibility, for fairly obviously reasons, existentialism became the dominant philosophy in the aftermath of World War II. It was the age of Camus, Sartre, and—

perhaps above all—Kafka. Communism and fascism along with their revolutionary agents were in the dustbin of history, or unwittingly headed there. Moral progress on a grand scale seemed a pious myth given the experience of Auschwitz and the later revelations about the Gulag. The aftermath of World War II produced a new preoccupation with the plight of the Other, with ethical responsibility, and with the rights of the individual. In deliberate contrast to the protestations of those Nazis at the Nuremburg Trials who insisted that they were just following orders, the new existential philosophy called on the individual to assume responsibility for his or her "situation." Such existential themes entered the popular consciousness not through philosophical works like Sartre's *Being and Nothingness* (1939) but through a host of novels, plays, and films. They congealed to form an ethos that is impossible to document fully or pinpoint empirically. This ethos existed, so to speak, beneath the radar. Even so, it would prove decisive for the new battles between the bigot and the Other.

Nonconformism took on a new validity and, among the cultural left, individuals were encouraged to assert their "authentic" subjectivity—and hence their identity—in reacting not only against anti-Semitism but also against sexism, homophobia, racism, and the Eurocentric delusions of Western colonialism. Inspired by *Anti-Semite and*

Jew, Simone de Beauvoir's classic *The Second Sex* (1952) called on women to fight their second-class status. It was greeted by a campaign of vilification impossible to imagine today. A similar concern with resistance by the subaltern appears in Jean Genet's work about transgendered life, *Our Lady of the Flowers* (1943), and his *Thief's Journal* of 1949 (which was dedicated to Sartre and Beauvoir). Sartre's *Saint Genet* (1952), a daring intellectual biography, highlighted the road to authenticity undertaken by his friend, Genet, a onetime thief and homosexual prostitute. Many of these writers also showed marked empathy for the struggles against colonialism and for those representing new social movements. Sartre's famous introduction to Frantz Fanon's *The Wretched of the Earth* (1964) and Genet's last work, his moving evocation of the Palestinian refugee camps and the Israeli invasion of Lebanon, *The Prisoner of Love* (1986), are testaments to solidarity among the subaltern.

Turning the disenfranchised and despised Other into a self-conscious subject and member of the broader community became the fundamental aim of political "engagement." Humanism as well as liberal and socialist ideologies with Enlightenment roots increasingly were considered inadequate for this undertaking. Their universal categories and philosophical assumptions were seen as ignoring the unique experience or "situation" of the woman, the homo-

sexual, the person of color, or the native. A new preoccupation with "difference" ironically came to emphasize
notions of solidarity based on the organic attributes associated with ethnicity, gender, sexual orientation, nation,
religion, or race. The idea of the universal intellectual associated with a tradition ranging from Voltaire to Sartre
now made way for what Michel Foucault termed the
"empirical intellectual."[26] That the subaltern should now
speak in his own name about his empirical experiences
was a laudable and democratic goal. But the primacy accorded the empirical experience of this or that group not
only often fostered intellectual parochialism but also, on
a more practical and mundane level, enabled the subaltern, in a self-serving and self-righteous fashion, to disregard criticisms or suggestions from outsiders.

Narrow forms of identity politics remain popular. What
today appears as a left-wing position, however, was actually forged in the crucible of reaction. Joseph de Maistre
put the matter strikingly when he wrote that "there is no
such thing as man in the world. In the course of my life I
have seen Frenchmen, Italians, Russians, etc. . . . But, as
for man, I declare that I have never met him in my life;
if he exists, he is unknown to me."[27] Many progressive
authors have cited his famous statement approvingly. But
it actually opens with the words: "The Constitution of
1795, just like its predecessors, was made for man." An

arch-reactionary, Maistre employed his empirical understanding of cultural identity (and cultural repression) against liberal democracy, pluralism, socialism, and ethical rationalism. He was a prophet looking backward. What bound people together, according to him, were the mythical, romantic, and existential "roots" that they share and that the Other does not. From the royalist-clerical counter-Enlightenment of the eighteenth century to the present, every reactionary movement would be driven by his kind of pseudo-concreteness and contempt for universal ideals. It is not the maintenance of "difference," ghettoes, or notions of "separate but equal" that are an affront to the bigot, but rather the specter of reciprocity. Hatred of this idea drives him to invest in notions like integral nationalism or the organic community—in which he has standing, things are as they should be, and all is right with the world.

The Cult of the Self was the title of Maurice Barrès's trilogy, which included *Under the Eyes of the Barbarians* (1888), *A Free Man* (1889), and *The Garden of Berenice* (1891). Virtually unread, and unreadable today, his books are interesting only as a reactionary response to the Bildungsroman, which was introduced by Goethe and other important figures of the Enlightenment. For many, however, Barrès's guiding impulses are still salient. He understood identity as anchored in intuitive feelings inherited from a specific social experience of the past. Only members of the community with whom the bigot identifies are believed to have the insight, intuition, or experience needed to make judgments about their culture or their politics. Emphasizing the "rootedness" of the individual in the history and life of a unique community, Barrès, Paul Bourget, Édouard Drumont, Charles Maurras, and others attacked the "deracinated" liberal and cosmopolitan "intellectuals" like Lucien Herr, Jean Jaurès, and Émile Zola, who defended the unfortunate Alfred Dreyfus, a Jewish army captain unjustly convicted of treason. The belief that reason is subordinate to intuition and prejudice in guiding human affairs, affirming national identity, and making political judgments is fundamental for the bigot and a cornerstone of the anti-Enlightenment tradition.[28] Those who deny their roots in favor of universal standards of justice are traitors by definition. Equal treatment for a Jew as a citizen of France will result only in further deracination and the erosion of its Christian heritage.

After World War II, when the aged Maurras was condemned by a postwar court for his collaboration with the Nazis, he responded: "This is the revenge of Dreyfus." The great conflict of the 1890s had solidified the intellectual connections between republicans and socialists even as it had generated the original proto-fascist movement Action

Française, whose ideology fused religious dogmatism, integral nationalism, and anti-Semitism. Notions like the liberal rule of law and human rights, cosmopolitanism, and deliberative discourse were treated by these bigots as conceptual threats to the lived life of the individual. Identity was, by contrast, seen as resting on a supposedly organic connection to a community whose unique discourses and experiences are intimately and existentially familiar to the individual. An apodictic form of knowledge is embraced that prizes intuition and resists what today is often termed deliberative discourse and the evidentiary claims of the other. Barrès stated this bluntly in his *Scenes and Doctrines of Nationalism* (1902): "Truth is not something to be known intellectually. Truth is finding a particular point, the only point, that one and no other, from which everything appears to us in proper perspective. . . . It is the past centuries which form my vision; that point from which everything is seen through the eyes of a Frenchman. . . . That is French truth and French justice. And pure nationalism is simply the discovery of that point, searching for it, and when it is found, holding fast to it and receiving from it our art, our politics, and the manner of living our life."

The bigot has always believed that there is *something*, some indefinable quality deriving from blood or nationality, that creates a special capacity for experience and belonging. The two are related since the supposed ability of an individual to experience the world in a particular way creates an affinity with others like him. This experiential capacity trumps what emerges in discourse or any ethic with universal postulates. Such experience or intuition, whatever is self-referential, becomes the bigot's privileged criterion of judgment. This self-referential position insulates his decisions from questioning or contradiction. It also creates the basis for believing in some hidden form of group solidarity whose recognition alone serves as the basis for authenticity.[29] In a famous 1925 essay, Franz Rosenzweig called this reliance on revelatory intuition or experience, itself generated from within a particular group, "the new thinking."[30] This great Jewish theologian of the early twentieth century, who wrote *The Star of Redemption* (1921), believed that ultimately such revelatory experience illuminates "my" essence and what it means to be human. But the "new thinking" is easily open to manipulation: it allows for a kind of mythical individual identification with the achievements of remarkable ancestors within his group (that is, with Einstein or Du Bois) that is at once self-inflating and self-deluding. This feeling of pride in ancestry is actually inauthentic by definition: it has nothing to do with the real activity of the individual in question and is thus unearned.

But that is perhaps the point. The bigot believes that

his identity, his upbringing in a particular community, gives him special insights and so the ability to judge others. There is no possibility of transgressing what Helmuth Plessner termed "the boundaries of community." Those who do not listen to the inner voice of identity—or, better, *his* inner voice—are traitors by definition. Reaffirming the bigot's identity calls on him to view reality from the standpoint of his faith, his ethnicity, or his nation. His intent is to restore the past or what Benedict Anderson termed an "imagined community."[31] Its allure can be as real for the weak and the exploited as for the exploiters. Insular preoccupations with discrete forms of bigotry can lead one victim of prejudice to denigrate the suffering of others. A certain victim internalizes the bigotry directed against him and turns it against the other: Israel has, for example, enforced restrictive housing codes against Palestinians in the Occupied Territories that are remarkably similar to those once used by anti-Semites against Jews in the ghettoes.

Competition also emerges among groups over who has suffered the most: Camus likened this phenomenon to the "algebra of blood." People of color can be racists, women can be sexists, and Jews can act like anti-Semites. *West Side Story* (1961) makes this point rather well. Ethnocentric, national, racial, religious, or gender prejudices are not confined to rich, white, male Christians. Conflicts between Latinos and African Americans occur frequently and not only among gang members. Enough primarily religious organizations representing both groups have hindered the struggle for gay rights. The target of bigotry can be a bigot in his own right. That prejudice is an attempt to assert social power does not absolve the powerless of responsibility. To deny this is to deny the powerless their residual and always imperiled moment of freedom Exclusionary ideology can take any number of forms. But it always taints anti-authoritarian struggles and distorts a progressive politics of resistance. What advocates of these exclusionary ideologies have in common is their willingness to dismiss liberal and cosmopolitan ideals in favor of narrow interpretations of group experience.

American identity politics took off after 1968 following the collapse of the Civil Rights Movement and the Poor Peoples' Campaign. Voices from many subaltern groups that suffered prejudice and discrimination started rendering identity ever more "concrete" through an ever-greater specification of subjectivity. Within the women's movement, for example, black women or gay women or gay black women demanded recognition of a new identity. Those voices undoubtedly deserved to be heard, but there was a price. Each repressed "voice" generated a new interest group or lobbying organization that was concerned less with broader forms of solidarity than with the needs of its own clientele. Whether pursued by the dominant or the subaltern, the strategy of dogmatic identity politicians and their interest groups is to foster the belief that those sharing the same natural or experiential attributes somehow fit together from the perspective of the "community" and constitute a target of aggression by the outside world. An unwillingness to countenance an exercise of identity (other than the bigot's own) is the core of the problem. The bigot defines the norm, and he necessarily defines it in a way that protects his interests.

Identity politics has been an important force in attacking "white-skinned privilege." It has fostered respect for previously marginalized groups. But the preoccupation with identity has also divided the exploited. Solidarity becomes insular, interest in other targeted groups becomes minimal, and cosmopolitan sympathies become secondary. In the United States the problem goes back at least to Susan B. Anthony and Frederick Douglass, when mutual distrust between civil rights advocates and feminists hampered both causes. In the 1970s and 1980s, too, as public resources diminished and a backlash began against the new social movements, ideologies expressing frustrated forms of subjectivity legitimated (often ferociously) the pitting of one subaltern group against another. *Do the Right Thing* (1989) by Spike Lee beautifully depicted the translation of all this tension into the bigotry of "the street." In his movie, set in a poor Brooklyn neighborhood, none of the characters of different ethnicities (African American, Latino, Korean, and Italian) actually listen to one another in their everyday interactions. Even after the groups momentarily unify against an egregious expression of police brutality, each is still ultimately thrown back into the same perspective forged by his own group, and life simply goes on.

No one needs existential self-validation more than the bigot's victim, and this subaltern can also puff himself up. He too can despise the unnatural outsider, the lazy immigrant, the conniving Jew, or the cosmopolitan intellectual. He can support cultural imperialism, terror, ethnic cleansing, and genocide or all of them together. The subaltern can cling to his own self-serving narrative, and he too will often change his tactics as circumstances dictate. American politics is littered with instances where blacks have been pitted against Latinos and against white workers, and white workers against women and gays (to take just a few examples). In their attempt to avoid universal claims and categories, as well as "master narratives," those promoting these damaging political storylines highlight not only the truly unique character of different prejudices, but also the empirical and supposedly concrete experiences of identity used to combat them.

What is true of prejudice between subaltern identity

groups is also true within such groups. Hierarchies have existed for centuries among Jews of different national origins, and American blacks have discriminated against one another according to the darkness of their skin. Racial conflict among Asians also has a long history. Patriarchal, homophobic, and anti-Semitic prejudices have been expressed, often notoriously, by movements that have advanced ideologies ranging from Black Power and Latino identity to the liberation of Palestine. This fragmenting of the subaltern is among the most important reasons that progressive forces have splintered. Each has an institutional incentive to privilege the concerns of its clients and battle other subaltern groups as resources grow scarcer and competitors multiply. Because identity is employed to justify the diverse ambitions of diverse organizations claiming to represent diverse subaltern constituencies, each can easily be played off against the others. Coalitions with other exploited groups remain possible. Nevertheless, the narrow pursuit of identity creates incentives to engage in what I have often called the moral economy of the separate deal.

The bigot is not incapable of solidarity. It's been said that 400,000 KKK uniforms were secretly sewn by Southern women—and not one ever betrayed the cause. But the bigot's solidarity is always with those "of his kind."

His notion of solidarity is stunted, closed in on itself, and beyond reproach. In this modern age, he is as intolerant and staunchly parochial as he ever was. But he has become sly—and he tries to cover his tracks. It is the task of his critics to uncover them—and, perhaps, what he is (consciously or unconsciously) hiding. Each identity generates its own prejudices; personal experiences can always be invoked to the person's benefit in any argument, or when the need for any particular self-definition arises.

The issue is less the analytic dissection of how identities intersect than the criteria for choosing between loyalties or dealing with circumstances in which identities conflict. And, in fact, the most universally admired movements of the subaltern have highlighted the principle of reciprocity. These were the movements led by figures like Mahatma Gandhi, Martin Luther King, Jr., and Nelson Mandela. In fashioning support, they often dealt with conflicting traditions within their ranks. As they exploded the bigot's stereotypical understanding of the subaltern, they also evinced solidarity with the more general strivings of the oppressed.

Only by embracing a critical perspective on identity can it become something more than an experiential given and a natural fixed attribute. Identity will then involve an ethical choice among what are often mutually exclusive (reactionary and progressive) traditions within what is supposedly the common history of a community, ethnicity, gender, nation, or religion. There is a sense in which "a culture that encourages its members to be aware of their own traditions, while at the same time being able to take a distance from them is superior (and thus more 'civilized') to one which only flatters the pride of its members."[32] Nuance of this sort is feared by the bigot. That is because it may imbue the Other with a subjectivity that supposedly only he can enjoy.

"Craving recognition of one's special, interchangeable uniqueness is part of the human condition," writes Melissa Harris-Perry, "and it is soothed only by the opportunity to contribute freely to the public realm."[33] Spontaneous action from below, the practical exercise of democracy, is the way in which the subaltern gains recognition and forces the bigot to take him seriously. Frances Fox Piven has noted that "the mobilization of collective defiance and the disruption it causes have always been essential to the preservation of democracy."[34] The struggle for liberty has always been the struggle for recognition by "ordinary people" who do not occupy the highest rung on the ladder: the person without property, the person of another color, the person of another sexual orientation, the heretic, or the immigrant. All of them have suffered discrimination that was buttressed by prejudice. It is worth remembering that the recognition they gained was in spite of the bigot, not because of his charity, wisdom, or cultural flexibility.

TWO

Mythological Thinking

Myths have always held a particular attraction for the bigot. They offer an intricate network of symbols and meanings for making sense of life even today. Myths express elements of a common human heritage. They evince desires, illuminate experiences, alleviate fears, and raise hopes. Mythological thinking provides structure. But it does so in a prelogical fashion that pays little attention to critical reflection or the transformative powers of human agency. The world of myth is fixed and unalterable even as it is often erratic and chaotic. It is a world dominated by fate in which one can explain one's woes without reference to individual responsibility. In 2012, after publicly amputating the left foot and right arm of four thieves according to their strict interpretation of Sharia law in Mali, for example, one of those responsible explained: "It is not us who ordered this. It is God."[1] Myths are easily adaptable to the self-serving outlook of the bigot. They are nonfalsifiable by definition, they contest modernity, and they rest on traditional beliefs—and that is why they appeal to him.

Myths enable the bigot to withdraw from history. He can view himself as a pawn of fate, of whimsical gods, or of other-worldly forces beyond human control. They invoke unalterable patterns of often invisible conflict between good and evil. Family, religion, and community are the points of reference for this fundamentally premodern outlook. The bigot has always employed mythological thinking to privilege his faith, his superiority, and his community. It provides him with stability. Disruption and unhappiness can only appear as a product of the Other's machinations. Mythological thinking builds the scapegoat into the bigot's conceptual apparatus from the start. It always provides him with someone to blame.

Having roots in the biblical image of a goat laden with the sins of the community, which is then sent into the desert, the scapegoat can appear in the most diverse forms: Jews, blacks, immigrants, Hindus, Muslims. It is possible to dwell on the particularities of this or that scapegoat. But that makes it easy to miss the forest for the trees. Prejudice is not specific and the scapegoat is a construct of the bigot's prejudice. Myths offer radically diverse images that can be interpreted in an infinite variety of self-reinforcing ways. But the bigot always manipulates them to serve his material and existential purposes. Mythical images of the Other easily translate into stereotypes that legitimate the superiority of the bigot and the validity of his prejudice. The inferiority or evil of the Other becomes immutable. Prereflective assumptions are introduced and then used to explain his experience, logic, or situation. There is no need for empirical evidence, historical inquiry, or even an immanent logic. Mythological thinking asserts what the bigot already knows. Truth is "revealed," not argued; reality is "disclosed," not analyzed; existence is "illuminated," not contested.

Mythological thinking is shaped by archaic images, folk wisdom, inherited claims, or traditional rites. It allows the bigot to privilege what has been preordained by God, fate, or nature. The cosmological character of myth provides him with a sense of how things should be (because they authentically are that way). Interpreting the world through myth enables the bigot to concentrate on what has already occurred or what is already known.[2] He thus finds himself in a revelatory world outside of language— or, at least, a notion of language capable of articulating the new. The future is interpreted in terms of the present and the present in terms of the past. Myth thereby provides him with a cognitive framework through which he can respond to new knowledge and information. The bigot is intuitively aware that different myths are constantly competing with one another. But this lets him believe that clashes between cultures or civilizations are built into the structure of life—and it causes him to dig in his heels all the more firmly.

Myth exists to serve his purposes—not those of another bigot. His myths are already laced with prereflective and existential assumptions that justify his views of modernity, the Other, and his own identity. There is thus a deeply self-referential quality to mythological thinking when used by the bigot. It demands agreement not merely on the abstract character of belief (God, race, nature), but also on the bigot's particular view of the phenomenon in question. So, for example, belief in God is meaningless to him without belief in his particular religion and his particular interpretation of its texts. Loyalty to the nation or community is similarly worthless without reference to the customs and prejudices with which he identifies.

The bigot always draws rigid distinctions between friend and enemy. But this is done prereflectively through ethnic, gender, racial, or religious stereotypes. Once again, assumptions taken for granted are endemic to the stereotype. They facilitate an image of the targeted group as a homogeneous entity: Jews are what they are, blacks are what they are, Hindus and Muslims are what they are due to traits fixed by culture, race, or ethnicity. Since the stereotype is always informed by particular interests, however, the bigot is always in charge of distinguishing between "good" and "bad" members of the targeted group. Thus the former anti-Semitic mayor of Vienna, Karl Lueger, could provide a penniless Arnold Schoenberg with a grant because he believed that the great composer brought renown to his city. When asked how he could support a Jew, he famously answered: "In Vienna, I decide who is a Jew."

Few concepts are better known, few are condemned as vociferously, and few are more misunderstood than the stereotype. It is not identical with abstraction, generalization, or the "ideal type" made famous by Max Weber. Abstraction is a necessary part of any attempt to organize empirical data; generalization is part of everyday language; and Weber knew that the ideal type, drawn from different expressions of the same phenomenon (say bureaucracy) does not exist in reality. The bigot, by contrast, is unconcerned with empirical data; he uses language manipulatively; and he believes that the stereotype is real. His prejudices and his interests become linked through his use of arbitrary and selective images inherited from a larger mythical outlook (whether in terms of gaining salvation in the future, preserving privileges in the present, or displacing blame for mistakes made in the past).

Not every stereotype is negative or demeaning. Claiming that most Italians like Italian food or that most Chinese like Chinese food is harmless enough. The Dominican Republic has produced an extraordinary number of great shortstops, and African Americans still constitute the majority of professional basketball players. The issue is not whether exceptions can be found, but rather whether the given stereotype insists that these activities exhaust the prospects and abilities of what a particular group can (or should) do. The bigot uses stereotypes in order to create his own form of ethnic, gender, national, racial, or religious predestination.

As important as the qualities the bigot ascribes to a group through stereotyping are the qualities that he leaves out. No other possibilities exist for these groups beyond those that have been identified with them. Negative stereotyping constricts the capacity of a group and limits its range of meaningful experience and action. Lord Chesterfield, for example, invoked typical stereotypes of women in the nineteenth century when he called them "big children." Inherently irrational with no aptitude for the sciences, too naive to participate in the public sphere, lacking the necessary ambition for business, and too weak and delicate to serve in the army, women were limited to the home and private life by the stereotypes used to define them.

Such views were so much the common currency of the

time that it would be difficult to speak of them as bigoted in psychological or attitudinal terms. But, still, they helped to justify any number of discriminatory policies and patriarchal interests. Given the bigot's belief in the stereotype, however, he could insist that these policies and interests actually benefited women—even if they didn't know it. And that is decisive. Women weren't asked and, in tautological fashion, the stereotype made it pointless to ask them. The same logic was used by imperialists in justifying their rule over colonial peoples who simply didn't understand the weight of the "white man's burden," their own inferiority, or the benefits that the West was providing them. Once again, the stereotypical view of the colonized made asking his opinion irrelevant. There is something important to be learned from this: when it comes to prejudice, self-deception is almost as important as hatred.[3]

The bigot wants a clean conscience, and he is given one by his imposition of predestination on the subaltern. Stereotypes harbor normative claims even while they justify privileges and interests. To put it another way, they mediate the relationship between myth and reality. There are different negative stereotypes but they all restrict the options, create immutable traits, and withdraw equality from the Other. Stereotypes were used in practical fashion to keep blacks (and other people of color) in slavery, in the ghetto, in an inferior status, and in segregated conditions. Because these peoples were seen as subhuman or as child-like, the idea of providing them with rights seemed preposterous to the bigot. They would not know what to do with them and, besides, the savage is happy with his lot. So far as the bigot is concerned, therefore, it is less a question of demonizing the Other than simply a matter of common sense.

Such is the argument made in the classic film *Birth of a Nation* (1915) by D. W. Griffith that depicts and celebrates the rise of the Ku Klux Klan (KKK): it is not blacks who are the problem, or who caused the Civil War, but rather the misguided Northern whites who naively instigated them into revolting against the natural order of things. With Jews, the stereotype is different. Their malignant intelligence has led them (secretly) to foment class conflict, exploitation and revolution, social decay and progress, economic crisis, secularism and the weakening of established authority. The inscrutable and deceitful Chinese, once derided as "yellow savages," also need to be watched. Especially when identified with the stranger, or the exotic, the Other is usually seen as an imminent or looming threat to civilization—as the bigot understands it. The point made by Pamela Geller's American Freedom Defense Initiative with its poster on New York subways and San Francisco buses supporting Israel against "jihad" is basically what the bigot has to say about every conflict involving him and the Other: "In any war between the civilized man and the savage, support the civilized man."[4]

Everyone can recount a stereotype for this or that group. But the bigot tends to transfer stereotypes from one group to another so long as his purposes are served. Arguments against allowing gays in the armed forces are not substantially different than those once used against women and, earlier, against blacks. Arabs, Jews, Latinos, and the Irish were all considered "dirty" in their habits and profligate in their sexuality. Invective becomes cliché. Stereotyping has a special affinity with racialist ideologies, which are usually justified in pseudo-scientific terms. These subsequently provide convenient shorthand for making sense of reality: "it is simpler to attribute differences to heredity than to juggle all the complex social grounds for differences that exist."[5]

Stereotyping is predicated on selective perception and selective forgetting.[6] Personal experiences provide the empirical point of reference for the bigot so that the particular is conflated with the universal. Preoccupation with this or that slight caused by this or that person in this or that group confirms the legitimacy of the bigot's prejudice. Stereotyping and personalizing thus reinforce one another. Neither gives a genuine insight into reality. The bigot's perception of immutable racial or ethnic or sexual traits is translated into his empirical experience of the Other: the empirical experience, in turn, justifies the general claim. The reasoning is circular. But that doesn't matter. The bigot's only aim is to elicit information that will verify his bias.

Thus multicultural education constitutes a threat by definition. It is not merely that alternate interpretations of the Other are unwelcome but that they contest what has been fixed and finished by mythological thinking. New cosmopolitan experiences, multiplication of identities, and increasing specialization are hallmarks of the modernizing process that leave the bigot feeling resentful and frustrated. He has no use for the cosmopolitan, the expert, or the scientist. They look down on him and, even when they don't, they intensify his feelings of inferiority and irrelevance. The bigot is better served by escaping into mythological thinking. Yet the lens through which he sees the Other narrows his vision of the world and his place within it. He isolates himself from what he doesn't know.

Whatever experiences the bigot has serve only to reinforce inherited patterns of thought and imagery. Seeking to restrict the opportunities of his victim, he ironically winds up restricting his own capacity to experience, learn, and reflect on reality. For all the bluster, indeed, modernity tends to weaken the bigot's sense of self and strengthen his propensity to embrace authoritarian politics. It is characteristic that "prejudiced subjects want to be taken care of like children ... they want to exploit their parents like they exploit other people. ... not being self-reliant, they need support and comfort, first from the parents and then from parent substitutes."[7] Thus they are easily manipulated, quickly enraged, and prone to acts of aggression.

The bigot justifies himself by employing the double standard: it is his stock in trade. Tabloids like the English *Daily Star*, the German *Bild Zeitung*, or the *New York Post* regularly publish stories about Muslims that would cause an uproar were they written about Jews or blacks.[8] The double standard, it should be noted, can be used to excuse regrettable actions by the subaltern as surely as by the bigot. Because an atrocity is committed in one place without condemnation or intervention it becomes easy to deflect the need for responsibility when it occurs someplace else. Invoking the double standard is simple and appealing. When marchers protested the targeted murder of black citizens in certain Italian neighborhoods of Brooklyn, just like in the South during the struggle for civil rights, white people on the sidewalks opposing the protesters shouted racial slurs and waved American flags. The bigot's refusal to reflect on the actions of his church, nation, or community is decisive. Exterminations of Native Americans, and genocide perpetrated against the Huks or the

Vietnamese thus have little place in the mainstream American discourse, whereas genocidal acts engaged in by other governments with other ideologies are mainstays of popular media. In a dramatic example of the double standard, Hitler often said both that given the circumstances he acted no differently than his enemies would have done, and that his contempt was never greater than when judging those "whose political aims—the fight for national freedom— were similar to those he himself professed to have."[9]

The double standard works wonders for the true believer. Orthodox Jews in Israel oppose being drafted though they are mostly staunch supporters of expanded settlements. They receive support from the state for their schools, synagogues, welfare payments, and health insurance. They also support the idea of required military service for all other Jews—just not for them. Orthodox Jews apparently feel themselves exempt from universal precepts embodied in the liberal rule of law. Insofar as religious institutions identity their faith as the only true faith, they allow practices among their own followers that are not permitted among their critics. Islam is no different in this regard than Christianity or Judaism. Allowing critics to utilize their rights calls into question the absolute and legitimates the enemy within and without. Freedom is always the privilege of the bigot. He can pray where he wishes, say what he wants, and pontificate in any way he likes. What applies to him, however, does not apply to the Other. Thirty mosques can exist tucked away in the warehouses, courtyards, and factories of Cologne, but building a large mosque for the 120,000 Muslims in that city is another matter. Certain influential German Jews and their philo-Semitic supporters stated openly that they "don't want to see women on the street wearing burqas."[10] They seem to forget that the Nazis weren't particularly enthralled with the dress of Eastern European Jews.

Resisting the allure of the double standard is a precondition for resisting the bigot. Outraged Muslims were surely correct in pointing out that Holocaust denial, or inciting anti-Semitism, is considered a crime in most European nations while insulting Islam and its Prophet is viewed as a legitimate expression of free speech. Such contempt for Islam has often led Muslims to engage in their own forms of bigotry. Responding to anti-Islamic cartoons by placing an $11 million bounty on the head of the Danish cartoonists or creating a contest to award a prize to the best caricature of the Holocaust deprives the subaltern of her moral capital. Using claims about the double standard in one case to justify acts of bigotry in another, or inaction when these acts occur, leaves the Other on roughly the same moral plane as the bigot. Solidarity with one's own group is easy—solidarity with the Other is always more difficult. Gandhi famously told a

Hindu man gone half-mad with guilt for killing a Muslim child during the terrible conflicts over partition of India and Pakistan to find an orphan and bring him up in the traditions of Islam. Not everyone can evince the humanity of Gandhi, but everyone can respond to the more egregious expressions of the double standard.

Experiencing the erosion of tradition and inherited privilege, seeking to maintain his sense of self-worth, the bigot has his own moral cognition. He interprets the world through myths that mobilize support from particular constituencies; he employs stereotypes and double standards to justify his actions; conspiracy fetishism becomes a substitute for analysis; and he is always susceptible to fanaticism. The more intense the paranoia, the more prone the bigot becomes to embracing apocalyptic visions of violence and megalomaniacal self-sacrifice. The bigot's particular form of cognition provides him with a way of understanding reality in a self-serving fashion and embracing contradictory ideas. It also allows him to transform an exploited subaltern striving to change his status into an inferior (or congenitally evil) alien with fixed traits. This makes it unnecessary for the bigot to revise his views when confronted with new information. Events always are interpreted so as to confirm his original assumptions. The bigot thereby becomes the hero of his own drama.

Conspiracy Fetishism

No one is more innocent than the victim of a conspiracy and no one more evil than the conspirator. The bigot has no interest in meaningfully engaging the Other. But he likes to believe that his actions are motivated by altruism or duty. The bigot has always been inclined toward understanding the world as a conspiracy directed against him and his allies, simple and honest souls, by evil outsiders and conniving intellectuals riling up the subaltern within what was once a peaceful, prosperous, and happy community. According to this view, there is no reason for the assault on tradition other than the destructiveness and evil of the conspirators. That assumption naturally only intensifies the bigot's paranoia, facilitates his projection, and inflames his hysteria. The more powerful the conspiracy, the more it is hidden from plain sight. Professional historians identify this interpretive view with the "furtive fallacy."[11] The more encompassing the conspiracy the more it can explain, the easier to mobilize against the target of prejudice, and the more extreme the violence that the bigot feels he can employ. Indeed, the more intense the prejudicial sentiments, the stronger the likelihood that his explanatory preoccupation with conspiracy will turn into a fetish.

An interesting expression of this outlook was offered

by Glenn Beck in a series of televised attacks on Frances Fox Piven that basically accused her (and her late husband, Richard Cloward) of everything from causing the bloating of the welfare state to bringing about the election of President Barack Obama to covertly planning the overthrow of the American government. She was an important advocate of welfare rights and the "motor-voter" bill that expanded the franchise. Apparently, however, this former president of the American Sociological Association and vice president of the American Political Science Association is still engaged in an ongoing covert attack on the United States. A quick look at "cloward-piven" on the web will provide thousands of references to this supposed labyrinthine conspiracy.[12] At the same time, the bigot believes that behind Obama are omnipotent interests like the Bilderberg banking group, the Chinese, the United Nations, oil interests, the Trilateral Commission, Freemasons, Islamic terrorists, Jews, even the queen of England—or all of them together. That some of these actors are influential is surely the case. But the bigot is convinced that only he, and others like him, are willing to challenge their plans to destroy his America.

Conspiracy fetishism involves something different than the commodity fetishism that Marx identified with capitalist production. Alienation creates a situation in which the real subject of production (the worker) has been turned into an object (cost) while the real object (capital) is treated as the subject of capitalist accumulation.[13] The relationship between the two is inverted, but both workers and capital actually exist. That is not the case with conspiracy fetishism. It also turns reality upside down: where once there was a secret cabal of Jews plotting to destroy Christian civilization, today the Muslim Brotherhood is supposedly planning to introduce Sharia law by infiltrating American government agencies. Press TV in Iran insisted that Israel was responsible for the 2012 massacre at Sandy Hook Elementary School in Newtown, Connecticut, that claimed the lives of twenty-eight people, including twenty children under the age of ten. Islamic fanatics meanwhile remain convinced that the killing of four Americans in Libya by mob violence earlier in that year was actually undertaken by the CIA to create a pretext for further American intervention in the Middle East. Conspiracy fetishism always provides the bigot with explanations for his own failings and the triumph of evil. It assures his superiority insofar as only he can divine the purposes of a plan and of an agent—there is no empirical verification. Conspiracy fetishism, in short, simultaneously turns the bigot into the ultimate victim and the master of the universe.

In the realm of conspiracy fetishism, inferences become facts; facts are arbitrarily fit into preconceived categories;

and counter-factual information is integrated into the conspiracy itself. The result is what Richard Hofstadter termed a "leap from the undeniable to the unbelievable."[14] Society no longer appears as an ensemble of social relations in which fallible actors confront one another and consequences often betray original intentions. Structural contradictions, mediations, and real agents vanish, depriving the bigot's analysis of historical specificity. Conspiracy fetishism instead highlights an omnipotent agent of evil in control of the most diverse (and often mutually exclusive) interests and seemingly incapable of making mistakes. The goals of the conspirator are deemed more apocalyptic, ultimately, than calculable. The conspiracy fetishist is unconcerned with supposedly superficial conflicts of interest and ideology among the alleged conspirators. Every problem can be ascribed to a single invisible cause and it is the bigot alone who determines the influence of the conspiracy on this or that event. His projections define the manipulative actions undertaken by the conspirators and, since only he knows what they are, only he can defend his church, tradition, or community against them. Thus the conspiracy fetishist emerges as the always imperiled savior.

Conspiracy fetishism is something more than belief in this or that conspiracy writ large. Our history has documented enough real conspiracies. Catiline's conspiracy did take place in ancient Rome; François Noël Babeuf's conspiracy of equals did seek to take power in the waning days of the French Revolution; communists and fascists did work underground to influence events; and collusion among bankers has marked any number of economic crises. Cover-ups have taken place and elections have been stolen. The current popularity of the conspiratorial approach is surely connected with the federal government's ability to exercise power against its citizens; the government's own employment of conspiracy rhetoric to justify its political aims; and its use of spying and harassment against critics and activists.[15]

Yet rational discussion of conspiracies remains possible if, like other historical phenomena, they are open to empirical investigation and the motives of participants are subject to debate. Then conspiracies become discrete historical events with observable agents rather than expressions of an all-encompassing plan manipulated by invisible forces beyond the characters involved. But any clear-eyed encounter with conspiracies is incompatible with the paranoia, projection, and hysteria that the bigot injects into his understanding of history. Introducing the possibility of a conspiracy in explaining a historical event is legitimate if there is empirical substantiation and if the interrogation of claims is possible. But admitting that conspiracies have occurred need not suggest that all of history is a conspiracy.

Conspiracy fetishism is another matter entirely: it understands any particular crisis or conspiracy as the product of a more profound crisis and a still more nefarious conspiracy. So, for example, Malala Yousafzai was shot in the head at the age of fifteen by Pakistani Taliban for advocating the education of women and, after being nominated for the Nobel Peace Prize, attacked for being a CIA agent and part of a Western plot to humiliate the nation.[16] Conspiracy fetishism insists that there is always a hidden hand at work and, in turn, this allows for the arbitrary arrangement of facts. The conspiratorial perspective brooks no opposition or critical interrogation. Questioning the existence of a conspiracy at work is treated as an emanation of the conspiracy itself. Criticism can only be the work of yet another naive idiot, one more cunning intellectual, or some evil outsider intent on confusing the authentic—innocent and good-hearted—man of the people. The greater and more intricate the imagined conspiracy, the greater in the bigot's mind is the bravery of the simple man—and the more apocalyptic is the necessary response.

"They" control public life—the banks, the media, the political parties, and the educational apparatus. There is no institution that "they" have not infiltrated. "They" tear the bigot down, prevent him from rising up, and thwart him at every turn. The sheer magnitude of the conspiracy justifies his pessimism. There is no room for intellectual hair-splitting, questioning, or self-doubt. Any questioning of the conspiracy is evidence of the conspirators' power. The issue is not that the bigot has real enemies, which he undoubtedly has, but that he is engaged in the millenarian "struggle" against an almost superhuman enemy. The more imminent and threatening the conspiracy, the less must the bigot confront himself, his neuroses, his choices, and the paucity of his ideas. That is the reason for considering the most grandiose of all conspiracy theories: the *Protocols of the Elders of Zion*.[17]

Conspiracy fetishism played an important role in anti-Semitism almost from the beginning. The bigot knew what was what. Jews had always refused to assimilate. They had always been pushy, and cheap, which is how they acquired their money, and why they hid their cash. They always seemed to run things. They spoke a secret language, read incomprehensible books, dressed oddly, paid obeisance to the pig whose flesh they would not touch, and prayed to an invisible (or better, nonexistent) deity. On top of all this they considered themselves better than everyone else: they called themselves "the chosen people."

Long before the Jews were blamed for the death of

Jesus, parables, rumors, learned works, and popular writings had already congealed into a tradition of prejudice. No anti-Semitic work, however, ever had the impact of the *Protocols of the Elders of Zion*. Among the most popular works of the interwar period, this pamphlet, with its fictitious vision of a Jewish world conspiracy, has waned in legitimacy but its influence has survived Auschwitz. Neo-Nazis love it, the tract is embraced by the Nation of Islam, and Hamas refers to it in its charter. The popularity of the *Protocols* in the Middle East grew following the 1967 war and again in the aftermath of 9/11.

Rumors still circulate on the web that "the Jews" were responsible for the attack on the World Trade Center. Only Jewish control of the media apparently prevents the world from knowing that Jews stayed home and that not one Jew was killed in the attack. The *New York Times* reported a more recent version of such thinking on June 27, 2012, when the vice president of Iran, Mohammad-Reza Rahimi, stated in front of an international anti-drug conference that the Talmud justified the illegal drug trade, Zionist gynecologists were killing black babies in Africa, and, with a whiff of nostalgia for the past, that Jews were responsible for the Bolshevik Revolution. Proof for the assertions is apparently provided by the (palpably absurd) claim that no Jews are drug addicts and that no Jews were killed during the Russian Revolution. But the empirical truth or falsity of the claim is irrelevant. Even if the bigot's assertion were proven false, he would claim that he has still clarified what the Jews were actually planning or what they hoped would happen. "They" performed similar acts before and, undoubtedly, they will perform similar acts again.

Conspiracy fetishism has a soft spot for melodrama. The *Protocols* were supposedly the product of a meeting in a graveyard carried out in the dead of night under the light of a full moon by delegates from the twelve tribes of Zion. "Who are the learned elders?" is asked rhetorically in the introduction to the first English edition of the *Protocols* (1922). The answer: "This is a secret that has not been revealed. They are the Hidden Hand." Or, to put it another way, no one knows who they are but they exist. Luckily the meeting of the elders was overheard by a good-hearted (if unidentified) Christian who made the world aware of this dark conspiracy. The gothic scene highlights the danger of the innocent witness. No one will believe him. Simple God-fearing people cannot possibly conceive of an international Jewish conspiracy that possesses "millions of eyes" and that, by the most unscrupulous means, intends to wipe out national rights, manipulate the economy, and turn Christians against one another through use of the intellect, science, and control of the press (wherein "freedom of speech finds its incarnation"). Darwin, Marx, and Nietzsche: they were all in on it. Enough honest Christians collaborated as well. But they didn't know what they were doing. The Jews always know. Substituting "arithmetical calculation and material needs" for "the godhead and the spirit," they use the press to get gold notwithstanding that they have had "to gather it out of oceans of blood and tears."[18] The bigot now has his explanation for secularism and the disenchantment of the world.

Conspiracy fetishism is predicated on paranoia. Jewish influence is supposedly completely pervasive. No agreement between nations or classes can be undertaken, or so it is stated in the *Protocols*, without the Jews having a hand in it. The ring of conspirators is closing like a snake around its victim and a universal economic crisis will soon throw mobs of workers onto the streets. "Remember the French Revolution, to which it was we who gave the name of Great: the secrets of its preparation are well known to us because it was wholly the work of our hands." The Jews have introduced voting and individualism, capitalism and monopolies, socialism and an invisible directorate whose principal object "consists in this: to debilitate the mind through public criticism."

According to this view, even the supposed enemies of this international Jewish conspiracy and its agents cannot be trusted. The leading elder of Zion states emphatically that "if any states raise a protest against us, it is only pro forma at our discretion and by our direction, for their anti-Semitism is indispensable to us for the management of our lesser brethren." Greed, ambition, vengeance, and malice are sentiments made for treachery. So it is that "we have in our service persons of all opinions, of all doctrines, monarchists, demagogues, socialists, communists, and utopian dreamers. We have harnessed them all to the task: each one of them is boring away at the last remnants of authority." Everything is covered up; all sources of resistance are tainted; the Jew is everywhere, and the best proof for the authenticity of the *Protocols* is the claim of Jews and their allies that the pamphlet is a fake.

Arguments of this sort rest on circular reasoning. But the conspiracy fetishist finds this irrelevant. The point is to take a stand. Those who cannot make up their minds have already made up their minds. The grandeur of the conspiracy is such that the bigot can predict his inability to verify events and that all claims to do so are, again, part of the original conspiracy. The conspiracy fetishist alone can decide who and what is relevant in order to make his case. Neither actually matters. It is always possible to invent new elders and a different scene for the conspiracy. The devil does not lie in the details—but in the fetish. The actual meeting of the learned elders is important only insofar as it provides an allegory and a cautionary warning for meetings that really took place like the First Zionist Congress of 1898 in Basel. So what if the protocols appeared in French while the language employed at the Congress was German? Hannah Arendt understood that simply insisting that the *Protocols* is fabricated is somehow beside the point.[19] The real question is why the fabrication is believed.

Such ideas still have currency. Rothschild, Rockefeller, Soros, and world Jewry were blamed by any number of religious authorities in Greece for that nation's financial collapse in 2010. The Metropolitan Seraphim of Piraeus claimed that this conspiracy was also intent on destroying the Greek Orthodox Church by promoting one-parent families and same-sex marriages. But that's not all. Coming on the heels of the international financial crisis of 2007 and the devastating impact created by the authoritarian turn of the Arab Spring, amid the Syrian civil war and the terrible domestic unrest in Iraq, the Middle East is experiencing yet another economic downturn. Arabs affected by this economic development surely feel a sense of humiliation and helplessness as they watch other parts of the previously colonized world—if only slowly and tentatively—improve their economic situation. The Israeli-Palestinian conflict and Israeli policies have surely contributed to the problems of the region. In the minds of many, however, the present economic disaster is attributable to "the Jews." This is not merely unfortunate for the Jews. Conspiratorial thinking of this sort so distorts the actual situation that developing an appropriate political response becomes impossible. In turn, this failure to develop a response tends to justify the original expression of bigotry.

The paranoia and projection fueling conspiracy fetishism enable the bigot to feel justified in doing himself what he believes that the target of his hatred is doing. The *Protocols* insisted that, like the Indian god Vishnu with his countless tentacles, "the Jew" was pulling the strings of a multifaceted assault on established society with an eye toward creating a dictatorship. But then it was the anti-Semites who were actually engaging in assassinations, bribery, kidnappings, and public disorder in order to destroy democracy. This was the case with infamous groups like the Thule Society in Germany's Weimar Republic and the Cagoulards in France's Third Republic.

The Jew in this scenario becomes anything the anti-Semite wants him to be: the capitalist and the socialist, the democrat and the communist, the educator and the bohemian, the homosexual and the starched shirt. That they might exhibit opposing interests is irrelevant. They are "really" all working together, because "the Jews of myth and rumor, then, are Virtual Jews, Simulated Jews— not real people but projectively constructed enemies, mythic abstractions from history. In the psychic economy of the anti-Semite, the Virtual Jew is a metaphor for other forces, the projection of other concerns—and is thus linked to real Jews in name only. This 'Jew' is a shadow in a dream world."[20] The *Protocols* enables the anti-Semite to reconstruct the Jew in order to meet any explanatory need. Because the Jew is a shape-shifter, a chameleon, simply restricting his rights or his mobility is insufficient for dealing with him. More radical methods are necessary. Better safe than sorry. There is ultimately—using the phrase of Hannah Arendt—no "place" for any Jew in civilized society.

Conspiracy fetishism is not confined to any type of person or any group. It can infect any member of any group: Hindi and Muslim, black and white, colonizer and colonized. That is because conspiracy fetishism does not deal with real people: only images shaped by paranoia, projection, and hysteria. "All things are lost to a mind thus enthralled," Ernst Cassirer insightfully notes; "all bridges between the concrete datum and the systematized totality of experience are broken: only the present reality, as mythic or linguistic conception stresses and shapes it, fills the entire subjective realm."[21] Conspiracy fetishism distorts the experience of reality, undermines the perception of historical change, and inverts the balance of power. The victim of prejudice can turn into the bigot and still perceive himself or herself as the victim of a conspiracy. Exaggerated Jewish perceptions of contemporary anti-Semitism, for example, assume that the entire world is ganging up on Israel (without cause) and supporting the claims of Palestinians. Certain super-rich Jewish hedge-fund managers even saw the election of President Obama as somehow tantamount to the reintroduction of the Third Reich.[22] There are enough Jews who think like anti-Semites—and are defined by what they ostensibly oppose. Note the language of intolerance used to describe the Palestinians by Jennifer Rubin writing for the *Washington Post*:

> Then round up his captors, the slaughtering, death-worshiping, innocent-butchering, child-sacrificing savages who dip their hands in blood and use women—those who aren't strapping bombs to their own devils' spawn and sending them out to meet their seventy-two virgins by taking the lives of the school-bus-riding, heart-drawing, Transformer-doodling, homework-losing children of Others—and their offspring—those who haven't already been pimped out by their mothers to the murder god—as shields, hiding behind their burkas and cradles like the un-manned animals they are, and throw them not into your prisons, where they can bide until they're traded

by the thousands for another child of Israel, but into the sea, to float there, food for sharks, stargazers, and whatever other oceanic carnivores God has put there for the purpose.[23]

Anti-Semitism still exists. It is, arguably, even gaining ground once again. But today Jews have their own state as well as strong lobbies representing their interests, and they have been accepted by Western society. Conditions are no longer what they were in the 1930s or even in 1948. Israel is no longer the country idealized in novels like *Exodus* (1958) by Leon Uris.[24] That is, Israel is not a tiny nation of settlers under threat from Arab hordes. It has among the ten largest armies in the world and it is the strongest military power in the Middle East. It has expelled inhabitants living in what are today known as the "Occupied Territories"; it oversees 5.5 million Palestinians living in fifty-nine refugee camps; and it is making the most of borders that remain arbitrarily imposed and not clearly defined. Israel exerts power over the Palestinians, not the other way around.

But the bigot is unwilling to admit that. The bigot's country is always militarily imperiled; his people are always on the verge of extinction; his culture is always in danger of eradication. Here, again, the paranoid style shapes the political message. Every criticism of Israel becomes an expression of anti-Semitism. Jewish skeptics are either consumed with "self-hatred" or misled by anti-Semitic media. Blood is thicker than water. The *real* Jew knows what's what. It's us against them: or, better, us against an anti-Semitic world with the Arabs in the vanguard.

Conspiracy fetishism generates an insistence on limiting the "permission to narrate" events in the Middle East to professional supporters of the Israeli state.[25] New research suggests, however, that Israel was never the product of a people without a land finding a land without a people. This was a fabricated myth from the outset; it is the same with the old notions of a national founding in which the original Arab inhabitants were peacefully removed from their land and that an overwhelming Arab force, united by its bigotry, was valiantly defeated by the "miracle" of Jewish nationalism. Then too, less and less persuasive today is the attempt to invoke the memory of the Holocaust in order to justify every reactionary twist and turn of Israeli policy. As the world grows larger, as other atrocities take center stage, and as the survivors pass on, the philosophical and historical meaning and symbolism of the Holocaust will change even while established patterns of thinking and plain ethnocentric prejudices inhibit the emergence of a new discussion.

Dealing with the anti-Semitic belief in a Jewish plan for world conquest is possible only if we admit that Jews are no longer in the ghetto or an oppressed minority. It calls for recognizing that anti-Semitism is entangled in a profound political crisis. Disentangling genuine prejudice from a legitimate critique of Israeli territorial ambitions should be the aim of all progressive inquiry into the problem of anti-Jewish bigotry. That project is made more difficult by the way in which Palestinians can be considered, using a phrase from Edward Said, "the victim of a victim."[26] But conspiracy fetishism and works like the *Protocols* clearly don't help matters. The seemingly immutable struggle between Christian and Jew becomes extrapolated into a new context as the struggle between Arab and Jew—to the detriment of both.

Anti-Semitism exists in the Arab public sphere openly and shamelessly: it is used to deflect criticism away from inept authoritarian states, explain economic underdevelopment, excuse past political miscalculations, and justify violence in the present. Conspiracy fetishism inhibits the ability to differentiate between progressive and regressive tendencies within the Jewish community and the Israeli state. It also subverts the ability to develop a sensible politics even as it renders any form of reconciliation impossible. Works like the *Protocols*—now over one hundred years old—thus still play into the hands of the most reactionary elements in both Israeli and Arab society, thereby guaranteeing only a further downward spiral. Embracing not merely its beliefs but also its assumptions can only produce self-fulfilling prophecies of the most terrible sort.

Fanaticism

At the extreme edge of bigotry lies fanaticism, and it is important to see how the two are related and even shade, imperceptibly, one into the other. The bigot is not a bigot twenty-four hours a day. He is not always a religious zealot, a contemptuous elitist, or an embittered chauvinist. The bigot is more than the role he plays. He can be a parent, a neighbor, a worker, a professional, a consumer, and a friend. He is often polite, hospitable, charitable, and nice to animals. His degree of obsession differs. Not every bigot is willing to sacrifice his life or murder innocent people like (just to use one example) Mohammed Merah, who in 2012 coldly executed a rabbi and three children at a Jewish school in Toulouse. Most bigots are content to shun the Other, brood over their resentments, crack stupid jokes, attend a rally now and then, and vote for the appropriate political party. Only the fanatic couples extreme paranoia with a kind of linguistic hysteria and a willingness to do anything for the cause.

Fanaticism enables the bigot to rob the Other of all positive characteristics, internalize them, and then project his own malignant fantasies back on the Other.[27] This double transference occurs in an extreme manner, for fanaticism exaggerates the sentiments of the everyday bigot. "Honor killings" deriving from feuds between rival clans or gangs, or directed against miscreant children within the bigot's own family, make this clear. It is the same with the casual hate crime. These acts occur within a context: the small town, the provincial community, the madrasa, the militia enclave, the ultra-religious community, or even the culture of white supremacy and neo-Nazism whose subterranean popularity is an open secret. Any of these contexts, though obviously some more potently than others, encourages the bigot to see himself (not only figuratively but literally) engaged in a life-or-death battle with the alien incarnation of evil. That is the point at which he becomes a fanatic who considers all means legitimate in defending his faith, his superiority, his community—and ultimately civilization itself.

Not every fanatic is a bigot, but every bigot harbors fanatical impulses. Mostly he tries to keep them under wraps. Sometimes that doesn't work and then his hatred explodes into violence. Fanaticism always muffles the call of conscience. Willing to sacrifice anyone and potentially everyone for his hatred, unconcerned with establishing any plausible connection between ends and means, the bigot gripped by fanaticism leaves no room for compromise, constraint, or the play of calculable interests. Violence is the enemy of politics—or the meaningful exercise of power.[28] Yet violence can have a lasting political impact. To think that 9/11 left existing power constellations untouched is to indulge in platitudes. Interest in the Middle East blossomed and the geopolitical importance of the region was magnified immeasurably. Not every fanatical act is useless or unsuccessful no matter how much it offends humanity, in part because crafting an effective, measured response requires returning to our moral compass, even when emotions are running high. There is no place in the progressive agenda for ethically misleading and misguided slogans like "by any means necessary." Any fanatic likes to claim that the end justifies the means—but he usually tends to forget that in real political life the only concrete justification of the end is the means used to achieve it.

Fanaticism calls for drawing a line in the sand—and only the fanatic will decide who has crossed it. Distinctions between the innocent and the guilty—adults, children, or old people—are as meaningless as distinctions between rats. Neither the suicide bomber nor the genocidal maniac entertains any meaningful difference between the Arab selling kebabs on some street corner and the agent of al-Qaeda, the Tutsi as soldier or the Tutsi as farmer, the Hindi in power or the Hindi out of power.

The fanatical bigot is as unconcerned with the standing of the foreigner whom he attacks as the rapist is with the appearance of his victim. There is only the Other who deserves the violence directed against him. Those unwilling to join in the violence, or who qualify the need for violence, have already betrayed the cause. That is true even of other (more circumspect) bigots.

Fanaticism prevents the bigot from sparing either himself or others: demonizing the enemy becomes a form of self-worship. Paranoia and megalomania blend in his mind. The bigot alone is standing up against some grandiose conspiracy. Whether it takes a Jewish, "mongrel," or "Eurabian" form is basically immaterial. Expediency determines the target: it could be a rival on the right, an opponent on the left, a doctor performing abortions, or a public building like the World Trade Center on 9/11. In the 1978 novel *The Turner Diaries*, which has come to be known as the "bible of the racist right," radical racists even bomb FBI headquarters and the Pentagon.[29] But then, Eichmann also taught us that the fanatic can be the guy next door and that the most extreme acts of bigotry can be undertaken from behind a desk. All that matters is the bigot's willingness to do anything in his enduring battle with the Other whose origins reach back to the beginning of time.

Hitler is a perfect example. He believed that fate had ordained him to lead an anthropologically grounded international race war. He understood World War II as a contest between Germany and its rival nation-states but also, simultaneously, between Aryans and Jews along with their other supposedly subhuman allies. Not only was the ideological race war carried on at the same time as the war between nations, but the "final solution" of the Jewish question was also undertaken just as the military conflict was becoming particularly acute. Ideology has its own logic. So it was that the concentration camps expanded precisely as it became ever more apparent that Germany had lost the war. Instrumental concerns associated with the actual military conflict became subordinate to the war against the internal enemy. The Nazis wasted trains, troops, and valuable matériel on this gruesome undertaking. Still, the less time Hitler felt he had, the greater his commitment became to the apocalyptic goal.

Calling for a rebirth of humanity, Hitler's *Mein Kampf* famously envisioned eliminating all races leaving only two racially pure Aryan specimens. The self-published *Turner Diaries* by "Andrew Macdonald" (a pseudonym for William Luther Pierce) has sold hundreds of thousands of copies (mostly at gun shows) and concludes with its hero piloting a plane with a nuclear explosive into the Pentagon amid an ongoing race war.[30] Anders Behring Breivik, who set off a car bomb in Oslo, killing eight, then murdered another sixty-nine teenage socialist activists on retreat in 2011, left behind a rambling thousand-page Internet manifesto that called for a transnational uprising against the Islamic "invasion" of Europe and the "colonization" of white Europeans. His acts of terror, no less than his unfulfilled desire to behead former prime minister Gro Harlem Brundtland, mirrored the atrocities perpetrated by Islamic extremists. But that didn't matter. The double standard was again operative.[31] Intoxicated by bloodlust, driven by hatred, fanaticism inflates the bigot's ego. Only the most extreme truly believes that he is helping avert civilization's decline by bringing about Armageddon.

Fanaticism always generates international ambitions. Hitler may have spoken about restoring German dignity following World War I, but he also sought to build an international form of Aryan consciousness. The *Turner Diaries* may have been set in the United States, where genuine patriots were depicted under the control of Jews and mongrels, but its "cosmotheism" (a mixture of evolutionary pseudo-science and racial mysticism) was seen as having global implications. As for Breivik, who was influenced by *The Turner Diaries*, he saw himself as a commander of the "Knights Templar Europe" and part of a pan-European "resistance movement" composed of groups like the English Defense League and websites like Gates of Vienna.[32] Hitler, Macdonald, and Breivik all called for radical solidarity across national lines in order to counter the enemy of choice. Each saw himself as igniting the spark that will awaken the masses. Internalizing myths, stereotypes, and double standards, they set themselves a tall order. Their fanaticism left them gambling on the apocalypse—and that is no recipe for success.

The fanatic subsists not on militant optimism but on heroic pessimism. Hitler believed that his defeat in World War II was attributable not only to international Jewry, but also to the weakness of his own followers; the selfless act of suicide by the eponymous hero of the *Turner Diaries* does not bring immediate victory or the collapse of the mongrel "system"; and, according to Breivik, the Islamic invasion has already gone too far. Degeneracy and decline are important words to the fanatic. They define a seemingly irreversible situation. Only an apocalyptic break can do the trick and bringing that about requires a cosmic vision, a cosmic hero. The odds against him are astronomical: the masses are too stupid, or too passive, and the elites have been corrupted. Success is a matter of luck—or destiny. Thus Pierce can write in the *Turner Diaries:* "For the first time I understand the deepest meaning of what we are doing. I understand now why we cannot fail, no matter what we must do to win and no matter how many of us must perish in doing it. Everything that has been and everywhere that it is yet to be depends on us. We are truly the instruments of God in the fulfillment of His Grand design."[33]

The fanatical bigot is a "real man." Little wonder that he should obsess over the imminent prospect of matriarchy or that he believes the modern woman is lessening virility. Feminism is seen as threatening the traditional family and preventing an appropriately high birthrate among whites. Traditional male values associated with power and courage, it seems, have given way to feminine sentiments like compassion and pity. These only impede men like him. They render the fanatic's struggle more difficult and give his enemies an advantage in the clash between races and civilizations. Breivik, for example, insisted that growing femininity had rendered Europeans unwilling to pass the harsh, yet necessary, legislation that might stem the flow of immigration and keep Islam in check. In his manifesto, he suggests not only that women should stay in the kitchen but also that birthing should be outsourced to third-world countries, genetic screening of the fetus should take place, and the state should employ parents to raise families of eight children or more. Feminism apparently undermines the ability of men to compete and dilutes the ideal of masculinity. The fanatical bigot's fear of deracination is interwoven with the fear of emasculation in a particularly radical way.

All this appeals to the little guy who likes to puff himself up. Images arise of protecting friends and family from the dangers of "Londonistan" or "Eurabia." The bigot's personal experiences now express something larger, something historic, something mythic and grandiose in their implications. The Jewish diamond merchant who may have ripped him off is symptomatic of a broader conspiracy and a deeper evil that only the fanatic really grasps. The Muslim lady wearing her hijab and yelling at her neighbor in Arabic expresses the enormity of the cultural threat—yet only the fanatic really feels the appropriate disgust. The black guy hanging out on the corner eyeing the white girl—only the fanatic knows what he really wants. The homosexual holding hands with his boyfriend while walking down the street—only the fanatic really recognizes the threat they pose to "our" families and "our" children. The fanatical bigot's mind is like an echo chamber in which his prejudices grow louder and louder. Drastic action and discipline are required to deal with a world poised to overwhelm him. For the savior on horseback, the dragon becomes a pretext for authoritarian rule.[34]

Fanaticism gives a kind of military stamp to the true believer, the elitist, or the chauvinist. The brand of ideology is less important than unflinching adherence to its teachings. Every revision provides yet another sign of degeneracy or decline. Allowing women to drive challenges patriarchy in Saudi Arabia; working on Saturday challenges the Jewish character of the Israeli state; providing condoms implies fornication and homosexuality. Absolute conformity, not change, is what the fanatic demands. He may be erudite, even sophisticated. But his obsessive rigidity turns him into a kind of raging automaton fueled by the thirst for revenge against the Other for supposed slights, insults, and acts of evil. The fanatic raises the worst qualities of the everyday bigot to a fevered pitch and generates an apocalyptic mindset that leaves him no reason to respect the cultural inheritances of the past.

The genocidal apocalypse envisioned by the fanatic rests on a desire to liberate the world from the idea of liberation and emancipate it from emancipation. As Hitler put it: "What is different must go!" The outsider's culture is incompatible with that of the fanatic—and the hatred he bears for the Other is merely a mirror image of the enmity that he feels the Other has for him. Projection thus fuels the fanatic's outlook. That is perhaps true of every bigot. But the fanatic is proactive: he acts on what he believes the Other is planning. Himmler employed this logic in his famous speech to the SS that insisted the secret police are the true victims of the Nazi race war because they must commit such enormous crimes to rid the world of the Jew. Similarly, in the *Turner Diaries*, the "system's" outlawing of private ownership of firearms will generate more violence against the fanatical bigots so that their strategy of preparing an all-encompassing race war only makes sense. Breivik believed that it was liberals and Muslims who were inciting a new race war. When his half-crazed writings showed the influence of American anti-Muslim websites like Gates of Vienna and Atlas Shrugs, Pamela Geller, the editor of Atlas Shrugs, responded that it was "ridiculous" to suggest that she or her "counter-jihad" comrades bore any responsibility for the violence: "If anyone incited [Breivik] to violence, it was Islamic supremacists." And for good measure, Ann Coulter insisted in *The National Review Online* that as a response to terrorism, "We should invade *their* countries, kill their leaders and convert them to Christianity. We weren't punctilious about locating and punishing only Hitler and his top officers. We carpet bombed German cities; we killed civilians. That's war. And this is war."[35]

Not every fanatical bigot has the good fortune to serve a genocidal regime or movement, but every fanatical bigot harbors a genocidal longing. That is clear in the thinking of Hitler, Macdonald, and Breivik. It is no less apparent in the "Caves of the Patriarchs" massacre perpetrated by Baruch Goldstein in 1994 that left twenty-five dead and wounded 125 Islamic worshipers in Hebron. There is only the bigot and his enemy. Differences among Arabs, Jews, or people of color don't warrant consideration. There is only the Other: ambitious, insidious, taking ever new forms. The fanatic and his friends are the real victims: it is the outsiders and minorities who somehow wield (conspiratorial) power over the state, the media, and the economy. Politics has nothing to do with constraints and opportunities. Thus the fanatic believes that apocalyptic action—terror on an unimaginable scale, nuclear war, worldwide devastation—is necessary to bring about the new world of racial purity.[36]

The fanatic is defined by the image of the Other that his parochial world has constructed for him. This is why psychologists so often find that bigoted fanatics, who are obsessed with charisma, have no personality of their own. Paranoia breeds the fanatic's hysterical sense of urgency that, in turn, intensifies his paranoia. His ever more intense fear of an Arab invasion, a Jewish conspiracy, or blasphemy directed against his deity allows him to understand himself as clear-sighted and normal and his critics as dangerously insane. After all, the bigoted fanatic is the protector of family, church, nation, and race.[37] Any effort by respectable society to marginalize him only further legitimates his condemnation of the compassionate, the pragmatic, the cowardly, and the weak. The more marginalized he is the more paranoid he becomes, and the more paranoid he is the more megalomaniacal he becomes. No one else can be trusted. Everyone else has been duped by the state, the media, and the conspiracy. Against them, indeed, the fanatic understands himself as the persecuted prophet of a new racially purified era, railing against the mongrelized world of modernity and ready to take up arms.

THREE

Playing the Role

The bigot finds it hard to appear as what he is: the old unvarnished rhetoric of hate is difficult to endure even for many of his allies and certainly for many potential allies. But the language becomes more palatable when used by the true believer, the elitist, or the chauvinist. These roles make the bigot socially acceptable and they serve to legitimate his prejudices. To be sure, he is still resentful and intolerant to the target of his hatred. His personality is still stunted and the bigot still, as Sartre put it, "chooses to reason falsely." But the particular rationality he chooses is intertwined with the particular role he plays. So are the bigot's sentiments put on display. The true believer can insist on his personal connection with the deity, condemn the heretic, and proclaim the absolute character of revealed truth. The elitist can insist that egalitarian experiments work against the interests of the subaltern and embrace the privileges and self-satisfaction associated with the conservative disposition. As for the chauvinist, his superiority rests on visions of an organic community in which each knew his place and for those good old days that were especially good for him. The roles are distinct yet they overlap. Each enables the bigot to turn the subaltern into the Other and validate himself.

Religious conviction, inherited knowledge, and communal loyalties fuel the bigot's sense of self. These sentiments, it might be argued, exist simultaneously in his psyche. As circumstances dictate, however, the bigot will privilege one over the others. Each lets him navigate everyday life in a slightly different way. Each has its own rationale, its own ideals, and its own compensations. Each provides him with a way of securing his existential worth, his social privileges, and his identification with the world in which he came to be what he is. All the roles played by the bigot buttress an "affirmative culture" supposedly superior to any other. The decisive characteristic of this culture, according to Herbert Marcuse, is its "assertion of a universally obligatory, eternally better and more valuable world that must be unconditionally affirmed: a world essentially different from the factual world of the daily struggle for existence, yet realizable by every individual 'from within' without any transformation of the state of fact. It is only in this culture that cultural activities and objects gain that value that elevates them above the everyday sphere. Their reception becomes an act of celebration and exaltation."[1]

None of the bigot's roles allows him to employ language as a medium for illuminating what is intellectually unknown: it exists merely to affirm what has already been intuitively disclosed to him.[2] As a true believer, an elitist, or a chauvinist, the bigot is thus provided with an entirely self-referential way of living in the world. Of course, none of these roles is exhausted by the ways in which the bigot plays them. True believers can work for progressive causes, evince erudition, and treat those of different faiths with respect and courtesy. Elitists often do prize excellence and their defense of tradition from the shifting winds of fashion is often laudable. The ability to discriminate is part of everyday life and, however unctuous or unpleasant, all elitists are not necessarily bigots. As for provincial chauvinists, their mode of life really is imperiled. Their concern over the erosion of tradition, civility, community, and identity is neither quaint nor foolish.[3] Faith, self-confidence, and even chauvinism can have positive connotations.

With the bigot, however, these sentiments are all given a particular stamp. He infuses any role he plays with his hatred of the Other and a greater or lesser degree of fanaticism. Belief takes a dogmatic and ostentatious form; self-confidence is tinged with hysterical fears of contradiction; and chauvinism takes on a paranoid quality. Theodor W. Adorno was correct in his comments about the role and the way it is played in society: "The concept, borrowed from the theater, hints that the existence imposed on people by society is not identical with what they are in themselves or what they could be. Certainly no simple division should be attempted between human beings as they are in themselves and their social roles. The roles extend deep into the characteristics of people themselves, into their innermost composition."[4]

Each role played by the bigot requires unthinking submission to what Sigmund Freud termed the "cultural superego."[5] The bigot tends to emerge from an authoritarian family structure, sacrosanct traditions, and an insular community. This comprises what Ludwig Wittgenstein once termed the "stage setting" in which prereflective prejudices take shape. The authoritarian family not only enforces sexual repression, which suits most religious and traditional institutions well, but also serves as "the factory" in which the ideology of an authoritarian community is molded.[6] It is well known, for example, that children who have been beaten by their parents tend to find violence acceptable in dealing with the problems of marriage and social life. Breaking the circle of authoritarian influence is a complex and multifaceted endeavor for which there are no quick solutions. But the connection is clear: where the authoritarian family narrows the range of acceptable desires, and authoritarian religion associates ethics with its rituals and dogmas, the authoritarian community narrows the range of individual choices.

Such is the crucible in which the bigot is forged. Whether as a righteous true believer, an insufferable elitist, or a resentful chauvinist, each role offers him the comforts of conformity and an illusory sense of singularity. His faith is an absolute faith and the only one worth having; his knowledge is verified by habit and experience; he is part of an exclusive community whose privileges he enjoys, and whose value is (therefore) obvious. There is a sense in which the bigot exists as a kind of booster or a raucous sports fan. His radicalism is tinged with the desire to appear respectable and—above all—to belong. His preoccupation with experience and intuition, along with his feelings of self-worth, presuppose the superiority of the community that generated them. To this extent, the bigot's subjectivity depends on his submission to authority.

Group unity and personal experience fuse in his mind. The bigot's self-validation and his identity are prereflectively internalized from his immediate environment. His choices are, so to speak, already made for him by his ethnicity, his faith, his tribe, or his nation. But it is important to note that the bigot defines his heritage as he wishes or, better, as it conforms to his privileges. He ignores the ethical, cultural, and political debates and conflicts that historically manifest themselves within his own group. The bigot employs homogenous stereotypes for making sense of not only the Other, but also himself. This refusal to differentiate between opposing intellectual outlooks or trends within a given culture, or identity, results in reification: the living individual is condemned to reproduce the stereotype that has been imposed on him by the bigot. In his understanding of identity, essentialism displaces reality and the bigot closes himself off from questioning reality's actual character and complexity. The fight against bigotry, then, should be based less on creating a tapestry in which each supposedly homogenous culture has its patch than on building a cosmopolitan sensibility that highlights differences not only between cultures but also within them.

New choices and ideas produce anxiety. In the bigot's view, only someone alien, inferior, or congenitally evil can possibly wish to deprive him of his privilege. The stage setting, indeed, prevents the bigot from testing or engaging with reality and thus from developing an independent identity and self-formative practice. The bigot suffers from a stunted form of subjectivity. He pays a price for participating in the cult of the self. Feeling his standing and status threatened from the outside, incapable of testing reality, his projection of guilt and responsibility on the Other is a product of laziness and settled habits. His world is defined by binary opposites: good and bad, black and white, gay and straight, us and them. With each new encounter of the Other, therefore, the bigot must affirm his prereflective prejudices. Resistance by the Other to this process requires punishment—and punishment requires power.[7]

The bigot's sense of self derives from what might be termed a power-protected inwardness. He cannot admit his failures personally, professionally, financially, or socially. All problems are displaced on the alien, heretic, immigrant, or outsider: the Other. Only in that way is it possible for the bigot to maintain his own standing and status. For him, therefore, it is always a question of who fits and who doesn't: what beliefs, experiences, and customs strengthen his standing. Consciously or unconsciously, therefore, the bigot will arrange his world accordingly, secure his position within it, and prevent it from changing or being challenged. His roles help him achieve that end. The true believer, the elitist, and the chauvinist reinforce one another depending on the degree of fanaticism. They shape the self-referential social character of the bigot: the particular target of prejudice is an afterthought.

How the bigot understands reality and engages society

stems from his social character. Some suggest that every social order produces the character structure necessary to perpetuate it. But this oversimplifies the situation, for there is a difference between what generates progress within the system and what inhibits its development. As previously noted, for example, prejudice is strongest among groups that feel imperiled by a seeming (if not always real) loss of cultural, economic, or political privilege. Ideas and values associated with modernity—political democracy, social equality, and cosmopolitanism—tend to have little appeal for those stuck in premodern jobs and living conditions, and those caught between the demands of large-scale capital and working people. Neither the KKK nor the Nazis nor the disparate groups of neo-Nazis nor the Tea Party were simply the product of some elite conspiracy. Certain capitalists or sectors of capital surely provided them with cash and expertise. But the mass base was already there. These were real movements and, before getting the cash, they were already pressing to be in the position where those in power would take them seriously.

The bigot is easily misled and manipulated—but precisely by those whom he trusts. The fears associated with a new multicultural society coupled with global competition and new forms of stratification generate a kind of communitarian nostalgia for the world in which he felt at home. Individual anxieties about looming changes are fueled by the socially induced obsessions of particular groups. There will always be deviants, and attitudes can extend beyond the groups and regions in which they were originally forged. Not every German was anti-Semitic or every Southerner a racist. But reactionary ideas appeal to some groups more than others. As Erich Fromm explains, while "the social character comprises only a selection of traits, the essential nucleus of the character structure of most members of a group has developed as the result of the basic experiences and mode of life common to that group."[8]

Enough thinkers have noted that the greater the homogeneity of the group, the more unqualified its ideological expressions. A situation thereby results in which the ego of the individual and specific ego ideals, which were established by the group, tend to fuse in such a way that the possibilities for self-criticism diminish as well as any potential sympathy for outsiders. None of this is necessary if the world is the fixed and finished product of a divine power that reveals itself to the bigot and provides him with a unique form of knowledge and justification for his parochial vision of community. Unable to grasp the historical constitution of reality by social forces, questioning the legitimacy of the claims raised by previously excluded groups, he introduces something wholly external and personal to which he—and society—must submit.

Whether it is God's word; experiential knowledge; or traditions handed down from the past, life is determined by forces beyond history and only in submitting to them is happiness or morality achievable.[9] The bigot is pessimistic about the future of his society, skeptical of intellectuals, and fearful of immense conspiracies that threaten to overwhelm him. At the same time, however, he is optimistic about the suppressed hatred for progress within his community, naive when it comes to the myths that empower his prejudice, and convinced that there are simple answers for a complex world. This ideological schizophrenia informs the bigot's identity and fuels all the roles he plays.

Whether he appears as a true believer, an elitist, or an angry chauvinist, a kind of hysterical frenzy becomes evident. The bigot blends into his role; he has no distance from it; he exercises no critical reflection on it. He does not simply make himself into what he is—he tends not to recognize what he is. The role is there to maintain his prejudices and, to this extent, he embraces it only insofar as it enables him to justify his dogmatism and deny himself the capacity to reflect critically on his condition. Sartre would say that "there are indeed many precautions to imprison a man in what he is, as if he lived in perpetual fear that he might escape from it, that he might break away and suddenly elude his condition."[10] To elude his real condition, to put his prejudices beyond criticism and change, is the purpose behind his presentation of self. The bigot revels in bad faith, he despairs that only for him "life, as we find it, is too hard for us; it brings us too many pains, disappointments and impossible tasks."[11]

The bigot's self-pity makes it tempting to dismiss him as a pathetic soul. But that would be a mistake. He also seeks to glorify himself to himself to society at large. "Instead of allowing his thoughts and acts to issue from social reality," the bigot "transposes reality in his fantasy in such a way as to make it correspond to his wishes."[12] That is especially the case under conditions of intense social or personal stress. Like a child, the bigot seeks comfort in a world that seems out of his control. The social roles he plays serve that purpose. They enable him, the little man, to appear as devout, wise, and a pillar of the community.

Even if the bigot is personally a "nobody," his roles turn him into a "somebody."[13] A representative of traditional institutions and values, he can now believe that his motivations are pure. But there should be no misunderstanding. The core notion of any critical social psychological inquiry rests on the assumption that what people believe inspires them to action is not necessarily what leads them to think and feel as they do.[14] The bigot does not simply bow before the moral injunctions of the establishment. His ambivalent attitude toward authority—rebellion against it when it hinders his plans, coupled with acceptance of it—constitutes "a basic feature of every middle-class structure from the age of puberty to full adulthood and is especially pronounced in individuals stemming from materially restricted circumstances."[15] The incoherence that permeates the bigot's character structure facilitates his ability to silence his critical faculties and, when necessary, the call of conscience. Theodor W. Adorno was right when he wrote that the scars of social repression are left within the individual soul.[16]

As a true believer, an elitist, or a chauvinist, the bigot's opinions are set before he enters into any disputation or engagement with the world. This fixed and finished quality of mind derives less from institutional strictures or overt authority than from a prefabricated idea of what is "normal," what conforms to public opinion. Freud noted the mixture of narcissism and paranoia behind such thinking: it affirms the bigot's self-love insofar as "any divergence from his own particular lines of development" is understood as "a criticism of them and a demand for their alteration."[17] The desire to protect his privileges leads the bigot to attack all who might complain or suffer from their exercise. But he is always anxious. The bigot has the nagging intuition that he is not making sense or, at least, that he cannot convince his critics that he is. And this leaves him prone to violence. Feeling "that something has gone astray in modern life," as well as "strongly convinced that he lacks the power to right whatever is wrong (even if it were possible to discover what is wrong), the individual lives in a sort of eternal adolescent uneasiness."[18]

The revelatory dogmatism of the true believer, the pretention and arrogance of the elitist, and the small-minded resentments of the chauvinist all contribute to an objective neurosis that generates feelings of ever more intense anxiety. The bigot feels himself justified in battling modernity and the struggles of the subaltern ever more fiercely. His resistance is predicated on stubborn intolerance and the ineradicable suspicion that his is a losing proposition. The same fights seemingly occur over and over again. Fearful of science and secularism, the true believer created a straight line that led from the Scopes monkey trial to the more current attacks on Darwinism in the name of "intelligent design." Elitists sought to preserve their privileges by vehemently opposing the great democratic revolutions, the burgeoning labor movement, anti-imperialist rebellions, the "new social movements" of the 1960s, and the fostering of dialogue among civilizations. The good old boys bear a particular animus against immigrants for refusing to abandon their supposed criminal habits, integrate, learn the language, and surrender old loyalties to their former homelands. The bigot is thus constantly shrinking his world, repressing his will to learn, narrowing his range of experience, and indulging his innocence. It makes him cling all the more obsessively to his faith, his ingrained superiority, and his vision of an organic community.

None of the roles played by the bigot is, again, reducible to his bigotry. They become identifiable with prejudice only when the bigot plays them. Just as the authoritarian character is defined by the attitude toward authority, and the sadistic character is determined by the attitude toward dominance and submission, the bigot is ultimately determined by the hatred legitimated through the roles he plays—and the intensity of his bigotry. Each role offers him a refuge from pluralism and the demands for democracy and social justice raised by the subaltern. Each associates him solidly with a group of the like-minded. Radical distinctions are drawn between the children of light and the children of darkness, the know-it-alls and the rabble, the good old boys and the outside world. Each role allows the bigot to stereotypically transform the subaltern into his self-serving image of the Other and, since these are inherently public roles, champion policies that would confirm his prejudices or, better, turn them into self-fulfilling prophecies. Thus the bigot reaches out to his audience.

When the language of intolerance fails, violence is always an option.

The True Believer

"God said it, I believe it; and that settles it"—so read a bumper sticker I saw plastered on the back of a truck. That attitude defines the bigot when he plays the role of the true believer. He wants definitive answers for the eternal questions: the meaning of life, the prospects attendant upon death. Modernity leaves him alienated and confused. Scientific developments and the expansion of the commodity form relegate the divine to an ever smaller region of the universe. Pessimistic about the future, the true believer insists that new problems require old solutions. His superior standing and his existential worth are certain: a proper reading of the Old Testament, New Testament, or Koran makes this clear. Citations can always be found that insist on the inferiority of women, the depravity of homosexuals, and the use of violence against heretics and blasphemers. Opposing passages with a more tolerant attitude also exist. But they don't matter. Important are not the countless words attributed to God and his prophets but rather those words that the bigot wishes to hear. Whether he justifies his interpretation through convention, revelation, or exegetical skill is ir-relevant. The bigot is uninterested in debate. Opposing views are heretical by definition. Only his view is an ema-nation of the divine and captures its unchanging quintes-sence. How to deal with the heretic or the nonbeliever has less to do with principle than expediency. To question the bigot's faith is to question faith itself.

Yet modernity permeates the world of the true believer. It generates ever more variants of religious faith and an ever greater plurality of lifestyles. But because he relies on myths, stereotypes, and other-worldly dogmatism, the true believer cannot make sense of them in secular or his-torical terms. Events are interpreted from an eschatologi-cal point of view. So, for example, the talk show host and former Republican governor of Arkansas, Mike Hucka-bee, insisted that creeping secularism and the elimination of religion from the school curriculum caused the Sandy Hook massacre. The reactionary preacher Pat Robertson explained Haiti's poverty and historical problems as di-vine retribution for the first successful slave rebellion, whose success supposedly depended on Satan's interven-tion. Orthodox rabbis often blame the Holocaust on the pervasiveness of secularism and the iniquity of reform and secular Jews. Looking back to God's destruction of Sodom and Gomorrah, there is not a calamity that the true be-liever cannot blame on the victim.[19]

Of course, not every religious believer has this kind of outlook. Individuals turn to faith for an infinite variety of reasons. Spiritual people search for an encounter with the divine. Others simply seek a congregation of like-minded friends. With respect to the bigot, however, something else is in play. What marks him as a true believer is less the intensity of his faith than the degree of his intolerance. Both in the Occident and the Orient there is debate over the degree to which civil liberties are operative, a civic culture exists, and a "sympathetic imagination" for the beliefs of others is taught.[20] The true believer's intolerance and parochialism reflect his unswerving reliance on the words of an inerrant Bible, an infallible pope, or the Koran.

True believers insist that a single religion, or a single interpretation of a religion, should dominate public life. The liberal state threatens not only the status of divine revelation but also the institutional power of its interpreters—the church, the synagogue, and the mosque—and those who benefit from their mythical and stereotypic interpretations of the Other. To the bigot, the liberal position on these matters exhibits a tautological element. It presupposes commitment to the values that the bigot detests. So far as he is concerned, proper religious devotion requires the submission of the Other to his rituals and his traditions.[21] In a pluralistic liberal state, however, religious institutions and their ideologies lose the preeminent status that they had in the past. The church, the mosque, and the synagogue no longer dominate public life. Each is now threatened with becoming merely one private interest among others. Such developments insult the absolute truth that has been revealed to the true believer.

Intolerance is as old as religion itself: European history is littered with the genocidal violence of fanatical true believers. But fundamentalism was a term and a concept first coined in the twentieth century. Its advocates are less engaged in fighting other religions than in battling the heresies infecting their own. Why don't they understand? It has all been revealed to the true believer: he experiences what Friedrich Jacobi, the old philosopher of the German counter-Enlightenment, called "immediate knowledge." Neither his knowledge nor his faith, however, is strong enough for the bigot to deal generously with those who disagree with him. His self-righteous condemnation of pluralism thus always sounds shrill. His reliance on revealed truth and immediate knowledge also make him an easy mark for the array of religious swindlers that in the United States extends from Billy Sunday and Aimee Semple McPherson to Jim and Tammy Faye Bakker, Jimmy Swaggart, and Ted Haggard.[22]

Like any good confidence man, the most successful evangelists know which buttons to push and which passages to cite from Scripture. Inspired by their charismatic presentation, longing for salvation and a re-enchanted world, the true believer is awestruck. He also has more in common with the rank totalitarian than he might care to admit.[23] Fyodor Dostoyevsky recognized the similarity in *The Brothers Karamazov* (1880) with "the grand inquisitor" who champions "miracle, mystery, and authority" so that his church can subordinate the masses (for their own good). Thomas Mann built on this outlook in *The Magic Mountain* (1924), when he fashioned his modern totalitarian character, Naptha, as an ultramontane Catholic contemptuous of humanism (and its platitudes) who has an apocalyptic, hierarchical, and collectivist vision. It becomes clear in these works—as well as from history itself—that no price is too high for realizing the millenarian aims of the true believer—and it is, of course, always the Other who must pay the price.

Dostoyevsky coined the famous line that "if God is dead then everything is permitted." But then again, everything was permitted the bigot even while God was alive. Tribal slaughter by the Jews (the "chosen people") was a hallmark of the Old Testament. War and jihad, whatever the various interpretations of the concept, helped justify Islamic expansion. Hindu true believers were no better when it came to the deadly conflicts that cost 800,000 lives during the partition of India and Pakistan. As for

Christian soldiers: they marched onward from the Crusades to the mass murder of the Knights Templar to the genocidal liquidation of the Albigensians and Anabaptists to the countless thousands of witches tortured to death to the genocidal One Hundred Years' and Thirty Years' wars that decimated Europe, to the pogroms and the imperialist genocides visited on indigenous (nonwhite) peoples from Australia to Latin America. Hitler knew what he was talking about when he insisted that he was only finishing what the Church began.[24] How the children of light should deal with the children of darkness is purely a matter of expediency.

True believers may hate each other, but they hate the liberal state even more. Liberalism rests on the assumption that process is more important than outcomes. Its purpose is not to judge one religion or one interpretation of any sacred text against another, since each can find in any holy work what he seeks to justify his claim, but rather to allow all citizens to believe what they wish and interpret Scripture as they please. Not every critic of liberal process is a bigot. But the difficulty of finding alternative criteria for adjudicating grievances or establishing reciprocity has been palpable. Even in a religiously homogeneous community, new perspectives and seemingly heretical insights will undoubtedly arise. Such developments compromise the true believer's monopoly on absolute truth. So he must remain vigilant. Anticipating the dogmatic and unrelenting true believer of our own time, Goethe noted: "Religion of this sort is based on faith that must prove unshakeable, if it is not to be destroyed root and branch. Every doubt leveled against such a religion is deadly."[25]

All controversies and debates are decided on the rock of the true believer's faith. His point of reference is always what he considers infallible Scripture and his correct interpretation of it. The truth has already been revealed: it is there in black and white. There is nothing to add. Those unwilling to recognize this truth are either ignorant or evil. Conversion offers the prospect of grace, and if the ignorant refuse to see the light or turn their back on grace, then by definition they are evil. So it is that the heathens or the heretics deserve what they get: Christians and Hindus are still subject to forced conversions by Muslims in various nations. Those of different faiths have always been an affront to the true believer. He draws an unyielding division between the saved and the damned and—ignoring Reinhold Niebuhr's famous claim that hubris brings evil into the world—the children of light and the children of darkness. The true believer is ultimately concerned not simply with being "right," but with being "absolutely" right. It is his truth—or else it is falsehood.

True believers defend their beliefs by any means necessary. Scientific thinking has little meaning for them. Its provisional understanding of truth always leaves room for doubt. What counts are the revelatory insights that science might justify. So the true believer will endorse "faith based edicts," pseudo-scientific research into "intelligent design," and more general theories of "creationism."[26] His arguments have become increasingly qualified and his claims have grown thinner over the years. What began as a robust defense of the biblical standpoint that the world was created in seven days any number of thousands of years ago (depending on the religion) has morphed into more esoteric claims that there are exceptions to natural selection and that nature is so complex that its source must have been designed by an intelligent creator. The true believer can now only protect his most basic and sacrosanct belief in his wars with science and secular rationalism. The true believer simply assumes the superiority of his faith. There will never be enough scientific research to overturn creationism, "intelligent design," or other such theories.

True believers who angrily resent modernity are especially eager to reaffirm the fundamentals of their faith. Their sense of existential worth is intimately connected with preserving the kind of society in which their true belief is privileged. They refuse to accommodate scientific progress and they always seem to discover new allegorical and symbolic justifications for their beliefs. Such individuals blur the lines of demarcation between faith and scientific, social, or historical knowledge. But they deconstruct distinctions in order to allow room for dogma. Kant recognized long ago that faith could coexist with scientific rationality and personal ethics or, better, that religion could function "within the bounds of reason." His concern was not with the abolition of religion but with the intrusion of religious beliefs into the realm of scientific rationality or aesthetic experience. Marx also knew that religion was not merely "the opium of the masses" but, just as importantly, the "sigh of the oppressed creature" and the "heart of a heartless world." His famous phrase has been misused and taken out of context so often that it is worthwhile to provide the passage in full:

> *Religious* suffering is the *expression* of real suffering and at the same time the protest against real suffering. Religion is the sigh of the oppressed creature, the heart of a heartless world, as it is the spirit of spiritless conditions. It is the *opium* of the people. The abolition of religion as people's *illusory* happiness is the demand for their *real* happiness. The demand to abandon illusions about their condition is a *demand to abandon a condition which requires illusions*. The criticism of religion is thus in *embryo a criticism of the vale of tears* whose *halo* is religion. Criticism has

plucked imaginary flowers from the chain, not so that man will wear the chain that is without fantasy or consolation but so that he will throw it off and pluck the living flower. The criticism of religion disillusions man so that he thinks, acts, and shapes his reality like a disillusioned man who has come to his senses, so that he revolves around himself and thus around his true sun.[27]

Marx understood that the abolition of religious feeling was possible only by abolishing the brutality of material life and meaningfully answering the existential questions that make for its appeal. Seeking to abolish religion by political fiat, which occurred under communist rule, was an attempt to short-circuit discussion about the reasons why people believe. Whether the idea of a personal god is philosophically or scientifically justifiable also evades the point. What Max Horkheimer termed "the longing for the totally other" speaks to existential concerns with meaning, loneliness, death, and salvation. The fashion among secularists and progressives of equating religiosity with reactionary attitudes and know-nothing dogmatism plays into the hands of the bigot. There is far too much talk in liberal academic circles about belief in the abstract and far too little about the behavior of the believers and the policies of their religious institutions. Whether religious faith provides a person with comfort in a miserable world is immaterial (except to him). What counts is whether the true believer is showing solidarity in action with the disenfranchised and the exploited.

Albert Camus insisted that it is possible to disagree with genuinely religious people without insulting or disrespecting them. Confronting the political ambitions of religious institutions to define and dominate public life, however, is another matter entirely. Intellectual trends deriving from the Renaissance and the Enlightenment are based less on some philosophical obsession with atheism than on fostering a form of public life in which each can follow his own faith—or no faith at all. For them, therefore, it was mostly a matter of securing the rights of the blasphemer and the heretic from the rage of the true believer (in power). That remains an ongoing concern: Holy Scripture has never protected the true believers from one another. Most religious institutions have only reluctantly (and under pressure from secular liberal authorities) guaranteed rights to internal critics. Without a liberal state capable of guaranteeing equal status to all religious faiths and the exercise of autonomy in choosing among them, or in choosing no faith at all, "freedom of religion" becomes just a phrase. Whatever the "catholic" pretensions of a religion, its institutional and ideological authority extends only to its own congregation.

The liberal state has a far broader constituency. To this extent, Thomas Jefferson recognized the practical issue involved with religion (and ultimately race, gender, property, and all empirical limitations on citizenship) when he stated bluntly in his text for the Virginia Statute of Religious Freedom (1777) that "civil rights have no dependence on our religious opinions, any more than our opinions in physics or geometry." It is easy to take the next step: civil rights also should not depend on race, gender, sexual preference, or *any* empirical attribute of adults living in society. In this vein, religion turns into a private interest and individual faith into a personal conviction—with neither binding for the public at large. The true believer, however, feels differently. He identifies his private beliefs with the public interest and seeks to impose his conviction on society at large. The degree to which the bigot can do so defines the kind of state in which he is living. Thus Voltaire noted in his *Letters on the English* (1734) that a state with one religion tends toward despotism; a state with two religions toward civil war; while a democratic order with multiple religions allows its citizens to sleep soundly at night.

According to these thinkers, the liberal state is a watchman enforcing the rules of the game: it remains as neutral with respect to the claims of opposing true believers as the umpire is between competing baseball teams. All participants in public life have their ambitions and, if only for this reason, even-handedness is the only way of dealing with any of them. The greater the number of religious participants, indeed, the more neutral the state must remain. So far as the true believer is concerned, however, this stance insults the absolute character of his faith. Pluralism reduces religion to just another claim. Opposing it thus also becomes a matter of institutional preservation for Islamic Salafis, or Catholic organizations like Opus Dei. The greater the demand for recognition by the heretic, the more authoritarian is the true believer's response.

Not atheism but pluralism is the purpose of the liberal polity—and some of the best religious spirits. Roger Williams, William Penn, Moses Mendelssohn, Mahatma Gandhi, Martin Luther King, Jr., and Archbishop Óscar Romero understood this. They were secure in their faith. But the bigot playing the role of the true believer is not. He fears the Other because his own faith is weak—it is simply a shield to insulate him from criticism and justify his definition of public life. Genuine people of faith are those whom the true believer does not want to know. Their strength he sees as weakness, and their religious tolerance he sees as betrayal. That is why insisting that religion be a private affair and pressing for an ever more pluralistic public sphere is neither blasphemous nor disrespectful. It is instead a call for the faithful to condemn less, listen more carefully, and perhaps—above all—heed the injunction of St. Augustine to pray in silence.

The Elitist

Some bigots choose not to pester the Lord. They take their superiority for granted. That is the case with the elitist. In this role, the bigot is always looking down on the target of his prejudice. He simply does not take the Other seriously. That can be due to his unctuous view of himself as a sophisticate or as a streetwise know-it-all. The bigot playing the elitist is not always an intellectual, an artist, or someone who is "upper class." He can also be the half-educated populist, the petty bourgeois, the provincial farmer, or the hustler who feels that women always want "it" and that blacks are cattle. This elitist is special, better, and thus entitled. It is only natural that his interests and beliefs should define the public good; those challenging him are inferior by definition. The elitist feels that he knows what he needs to know—even if he knows nothing at all. He is smug, resentful, and dismissive of those suffering the brunt of his judgments or the actions undertaken while he and his people were in charge.

Encounters with the Other always seem to go awry—and why inconvenience his bigoted friends by expanding the conversation? The less advantaged, less talented, or those destined for low-paying jobs have no need for education beyond high school anyway (and even less for instruction in the liberal arts).[28] "All the decent draperies of life are to be torn off," wrote Edmund Burke amid the French Revolution.[29] As far as the elitist is concerned, the source of that desecration—the collapse of culture and a well-ordered society in which each knows his place—is, obviously, the Other. The conservative outlook thus overlaps with that of the bigot as an elitist. Make no mistake: Even the populist playing the superiority game can parrot the elite sophisticate who historically "has favored liberty for the higher order and constraint for the lower."[30] Or better, for those not like us—not as cultured, not as experienced, and not as wise about "real life"—but who still insist on becoming like us and participating in the task of changing what is (obviously) our world.

The subaltern is seen as lacking the old-fashioned virtues associated with the Protestant ethic—sexual repression and delayed gratification, frugality and responsibility, hard work and family loyalty—and that is what the bigot believes should keep the Other in her place. But social habits are shaped by how people live: the type of work and educational opportunities available to them and the despair that accompanies the erosion of real-life prospects.[31] The elitist's treatment of a "nihilistic culture" as the primary "cause" of poverty rather than as an adaptation to it enables him to avoid dealing with structural imbalances of social and economic power. This view is also fueled by his belief in the inherent inferiority of the subaltern—and confirms it. Symbolic predispositions toward prejudice mix with neoconservative ideas on the welfare state. Arguments against compensatory policies like affirmative action thereby often become both confused and exaggerated.[32] This is in line with the bigot's hysteria and indulgence in projection. Critics often simultaneously claim that affirmative action has had no meaningful positive impact and that it has become anachronistic since racism is no longer an issue (which is also patently false). In fact, it has been so successful that it is supposedly white people who now suffer from unfair educational benefits and the preferential hiring of minorities.[33]

In the bigot's view, liberals, socialists, and the subaltern seem to be fighting against the natural order of things. Things are the way they are and they are that way for a reason. The idea of a "natural aristocracy," whether employed by Thomas Jefferson, Edmund Burke, or unqualified reactionaries, has always been used to restrict the public sphere. To speak of educational progress, pluralism, toleration, and the like shows nothing more than an inability to comprehend human nature. The natural aristocracy is obviously composed of white men of property and the "white man's burden" was a logical outgrowth of this belief. The naked savage shall receive the supposed benefits of white Christian civilization—whether he wants them or not. Uncivilized savages are obviously incapable of making a decision.

Writ large is the real choice that the bigot offers the Other: conform or die. And if they die like flies, it only attests to their inherent inferiority. Their subordinate status was predestined or, due to their primitive habits, their own fault. So it was that elitists denied self-determination to most of the globe until they were forced to change their minds through often violent struggles that, once again, testified to the subaltern's uncivilized character. Prejudice for the elitist is simply sensible and, as a consequence, it is silly to "contemplate any other future for the world than its progressive Europeanization."[34]

Elitists can appear worldly and erudite but they are, ultimately, self-serving and parochial jailers intent on keeping the inmates in their appropriate cells. If the elitist is (grudgingly) willing to grant each culture its customs, there is nonetheless little to be learned from the Other: let him rot in his ghetto. The bigot may have his faults, but those of the Other are always more egregious. The elitist has his culture and the Other might have hers. But that of the elitist is somehow always better: each can have his truth but that of the elitist is always more compelling. Besides it is the elitist alone who is worthy of deciding on cultural and political matters. Elitists always insist on controlling the field of symbolic representation. The degree to which they exercise that control is the degree to which they can keep the cultural level from dropping and (far more important) their privileges from vanishing. The elitist thus actually relies neither on erudition nor information but rather on an imposition of opinion that always refers back to his tastes and prejudices. He defines the traditions that he claims define him (and the Other). That the logic is circular doesn't matter. Those seeking to challenge his control over the legitimate definition of cultural tradition instantly turn into the barbarians at the gate.

The elitist considers himself the guardian of standards and, against the subaltern wishing to influence their definition, the prophet warning about their impending decline. His skepticism regarding participation of the masses in public life rests on his belief that history has been shaped by elites or "great men." Desire for a charismatic leader has always been part of the elitist's response to democracy, beginning with Napoleon Bonaparte's abolition of the First Republic. This longing was evident in the French Third Republic and the Weimar Republic that Hitler and the Nazis destroyed. Not every authoritarian or fascist is a bigot, but every authoritarian or fascist helps create the conditions in which bigotry can thrive. Even if inspired by elitism, however, genuine movements that attack the economic and political system are necessarily themselves mass movements. It is therefore a matter of convincing the racial or national base, whose members are everyday people, to identify vicariously with the greatness of the great man and ideologically define themselves as the elite. Thus a character in Sartre's novel dealing with the 1930s, *The Age of Reason* (1945), insists that "in order not to be like anyone else one must do what everyone else does." Little wonder that this character should turn into a fascist.

The elitist's cynicism (or hypocrisy) enables him to align easily with the stronger party: it allows him to feel special even though he has done nothing special at all. Successful racist and anti-Semitic movements have always enabled members of the mob to consider themselves elites. Community spirit, faith, and patriotism can all be manipulated for that purpose: such is the sense in which Samuel Johnson stated that "patriotism is the last refuge of a scoundrel." He who conforms becomes something special—so long as he thinks himself special. The criterion of judgment is never what the individual does but how he feels about himself and the way he situates himself in the network of significations that define his world. This inward turn enables the elitist both to admonish the activist and adjust his own position as circumstances dictate. As

Friedrich Pollack explains, "By distancing oneself in such a way from the opinion and passing it off as somebody else's, a speaker can adhere to it in case of agreement from the group, while possible objections can be neutralized by retreating from the referenced opinion without consequences."[35]

The elitist evinces a conservative disposition that tends to differentiate him from a counter-revolutionary.[36] Of course, when faced with a choice between the left-wing and right-wing rabble, his choice is usually assured. The elitist has a pat answer for every question and he dislikes change—especially when it threatens his comfort. Compensatory and remedial programs targeting the subaltern are a waste of time. The elitist has no use for experiments that challenge tradition. That his knowledge harbors a self-serving interest is less important to him than the "imperatives of argument" that he employs to justify his beliefs.[37] If they rarely highlight his worst prejudices, they do provide a context for them.

It remains important to scrutinize the shared assumptions of the bigoted elitist and reactionary ideologues; there are points of convergence even between establishmentarian conservatism and fascist radicalism. Both seek to limit the public participation of the subaltern. Mythical clichés, sanctified traditions, and socially ingrained stereotypes serve the resistance to such progress. The clichés are taken as true, the traditions reflect the power of experience, and the stereotypes are shaped to support established privileges. The extraordinary scenes from Griffith's *Birth of a Nation* of newly freed slaves taking over the state assembly and peremptorily legislating the right to interracial marriage and other "crazy" egalitarian laws—half drunk, shoeless feet on the desk, carried away by their own propaganda, and contemptuous of their (white) betters—is illustrative of the elitist's attitudes. "They" cannot handle freedom. The bigot *knows* that. He lives in the real world—not the world of liberals and intellectual dreamers.

"Experience" shows that experiments with egalitarian reform and revolution have produced only chaos and anarchy. It makes no sense to talk about extending democracy from the civil to the political and, ultimately, the economic spheres of life. The idea rubs the bigot against the grain. He wants to have it both ways. He wishes to claim that his views reflect those of the masses insofar as he is embedded in real life even while his knowledge of real life makes him a member of the elite. As part of the elite he can look down on the (ignorant) masses while as part of the mass, he can challenge the (intellectual and liberal) elite. Totalitarians have always manipulated this particular psychological dynamic to excellent political effect. Nevertheless the elitist actually employs rhetorical strategies similar to those of more respectable reactionaries who consider the progressive's desire for change perverse, futile, or dangerous.

There is something esoteric about attempts to distinguish between these three arguments. All of them assume a false objectivity that makes it unnecessary to ask the Other his opinion or illuminate the conflicting interests between the elitist and the target of his prejudice in making a political judgment. Nature simply renders nurture futile. No revolution and no reform can change what the elitist considers unchangeable reality. He has already stripped great events like the English, American, or French revolutions of their radicalism and interpreted them in terms of deeper laws that validate his prejudices. It might be suggested that the perversity and the futility thesis are mutually exclusive since there is an apparent contradiction in claiming simultaneously that disastrous consequences will result from good intentions and that nothing ever changes. Those insisting on the perversity of reform usually rely on mythic narratives of historical development, while those maintaining that it is futile highlight the prefabricated hierarchical structure of existence.

Such nitpicking misses the point. For the elitist, the perversity of social change fuses with its futility: nothing really changes the standing of the Other; reform is futile and its perversity lies in not recognizing that well-intentioned experiments actually make things worse (for the bigot). Enough reactionary thinkers, however, have tended to fuse mythical with scientific forms of explanation: empirical evidence has always been secondary for racist philosophers and anyway, if required, the elitist will manipulate it to buttress the original prejudice.

What is often termed confirmation bias enters into the evaluative procedure. A category like intelligence or normality, for example, is first defined so that it conforms to the bigot's prejudice and only then is empirical evidence found to justify its validity. That has been the case with various forms of intelligence testing, which harbors class and racial bias. In addition, it is difficult to deny that many supposedly neutral arguments opposing gay marriage are fueled by an underlying anti-gay animus.[38]

Usually the elitist's arguments about the futility of change are both circular and self-serving. The elitist soberly observes that attempts to extend democracy or equality tend to jeopardize whatever progress has already been achieved. An ancient liberty preserved, so far as he is concerned, is more valuable than a new liberty proposed. Such arguments assume, however, the existence of a rigid zero-sum narrative in which the extension of one universal imperils a preexisting right. Neither the welfare state nor the extension of suffrage, moreover, caused any noticeable harm to civil liberties. Extending suffrage to women in 1919 or to Southern blacks with the Voting Rights Act of 1965 did not undermine suffrage for white men any more than legislating the right to a minimum wage undercut the right to free speech. But again, the bigot's rhetorical strategy should not be taken at face value: his concern is actually less with the prospect of imperiling rights already achieved than with the privileges that he enjoys. For his part, of course, the elitist will insist that he is only trying to help the victim of prejudice. But the helping hand is extended without consulting the subaltern. That is unnecessary. The elitist always knows better. Nevertheless, what he really knows is merely that the resentment of people like him will increase with each reform and thereby, perhaps, engender a backlash.

Explicit claims concerning the inherent superiority of a given race, gender, or ethnicity no longer openly enter into these forms of reactionary rhetoric. Religious zealots still wish to convert the nonbeliever or engage in some jihad or another. Some half-wit social scientist or another will develop his database and offer statistics proving the inferiority of the Other, cautioning women against studying mathematics, say, or justifying imperialism. But there are no longer the inspiring intellectual bigots of times past like the once celebrated novelist Maurice Barrès or Houston Stewart Chamberlain, the famous turn-of-the-twentieth-century racist philosopher of history who inspired the Nazis, or even the occasional great artist like

Richard Wagner or T. S. Eliot or a poet like Gertrude Stein. The elitist today feels bereft and lonely. He provides cautionary warnings about the decline of the West. But the alienation he experiences often leads him to the fringes of political life.

Mainstream engagements with the rhetoric of reaction tend to ignore this possibility. Most think of the bigoted elitist simply as a staid conservative speaking in stentorian tones with an air that makes his arguments seem more acceptable and middle-of-the-road than they actually are. It is easy to forget the deceit and the violence that have become so much a part of elitist politics (and bigotry) since 9/11. Commentators subsequently fall into the trap of taking the elitist's intellectual presumptions seriously, thereby obscuring from the audience the impulses that originally motivated his rhetorical devices. As usual, when it comes to the prejudices, the elitist's justifications shift seamlessly from one target in the cluster to another. He simply looks down on all of them and stigmatizes different groups (often with the same stereotype) as he pleases. Chinese, Italians, and Poles have all been characterized at different times as sly, stupid, dirty, and lazy. American racists have traditionally accused people of color of being sexual predators, but Nazis thought of Jews in the same way. Many believe that homosexuals should not be allowed to teach in schools for that very reason or to share the same foxholes as straight members of the military, even though similar challenges must occur when straight men and women work together in combat roles.

So far as the elitist is concerned, the recurrence of stereotypes only further confirms his experience of real life that, in turn, confirms his prejudices. In *Dusk of Dawn: An Essay toward an Autobiography of a Race Concept* (1940), W. E. B. Du Bois writes about being a student in Berlin and about his teacher, the famous nationalist historian Heinrich von Treitschke, who coined the notorious phrase: "The Jews are our misfortune!" Like most bigots, Treitschke held a cluster of prejudices. As Du Bois recounts the story: "'Mulattoes, [Treitschke] thundered, are inferior.' I almost felt his eyes boring into me, although probably he had not noticed me. 'They feel themselves inferior!'"[39]

Emphasis on the reactionary's imperatives of argument fails to capture his prereflective judgment or, perhaps more importantly, the way in which the opinion of the Other is ignored. To this extent, indeed, the issue is not simply that the elitist lacks knowledge of the Other. As Salmon Akhtar explains, "Prejudice frequently exists despite our knowing the facts. Lack of knowledge often plays a lesser role than the active jettisoning of available information that does not support one's emotionally needed convictions and plans. It is more often a matter of ignoring than ignorance."[40]

Even so, the elitist believes that he is nobody's fool. Irving Kristol once said that a neoconservative is really a "liberal who has been mugged by reality." Everyone knew what he meant. Kristol's quip fit into a preexisting emotional matrix of prejudice with linguistic and cultural points of reference that include "limousine liberals" and black criminals ripping off the welfare system. They are merely rhetorical variations of apophasis—the mentioning of something while denying the intention to mention it. Kristol's indirection and inflection deny the supposedly objective and obvious character of his statement. The audience senses what is being said: the insinuation exists in the midst of the disclaimer.[41] Perhaps there never was an imperative of argument to begin with—only a preexisting prejudice cloaked in speech. This is when it becomes most apparent that the elitist is less concerned with the imperatives of argument, or logic, than the simple ability to exercise power over the discourse.

What matters is that the wisdom of the elitist is confirmed. Indifference to the public good in the name of irrational and dogmatic principles is always projected on the cosmopolitan, the liberal, and the intellectual. That is why their repudiations of prejudice always ring hollow in the ears of the genuinely bigoted elitist. If violence is introduced into the equation, then that is not the work of those at the top of the hierarchy (or who believe that they are or should be) but of the subaltern who—by definition—cannot possibly understand how politics "really" works. The propensity toward violence occurs because the subaltern (inherently) lacks common sense, because his emotions get in the way, and because he resents his betters.

Except for the violence generated by colonialism and imperialism, of course, the real culprit has mostly been the "insider"—not the "outsider." For all the stereotypes employed by the elitist about African Americans, indeed, noteworthy is what the elitist tends to forget, namely, how black people generally abstained from violence in response to the bigotry and oppression they experienced throughout American history. Not the subaltern but the hegemonic power is usually the source of violence.[42] Gay people know this well: so do the female victims of incest, rape, and spousal abuse; Native Americans; and African Americans. There is something deeply perverse about the elitist's fear of violence by the Other and his own willingness to use it in order to protect his community and public life from the uncivilized rabble.

Not the elitist's education, not his tastes, not his language, not his status, but his unyielding contempt for the inherently inferior Other marks him as a bigot. He is unconcerned with righting past wrongs or compensating the subaltern for historical maltreatment. The elitist benefits from the existing imbalance of economic and social power. And he is intent on denying recognition to those wishing to transform it. The integration of the marginalized and disenfranchised into public life has always been seen by the bigoted elitist as an insult to his cultural standing: it smacks of what Barrès liked to call a "deracinated hubris." Thus the line appears in the sand between the true believer and the pluralist, the elitist and the democrat, and—ultimately—the cosmopolitan and the chauvinist.

The Chauvinist

Some bigots claim divine revelation to justify their superiority. Others require compelling imperatives of argument. But the bigot in the guise of the chauvinist needs only a self-serving narrative of belonging. This narrative is fueled by nostalgia for the past—or, better, what the bigot imagines the past must have been. It is a narrative in which the Other disappears: or better, the exploitation and discrimination he suffers disappear. Bringing up the Other's persecution would only disrupt the narrative. Such is the meaning behind the belief still current in the American South: "It's not a matter of race but of heritage." European neofascist leaders would probably agree. They, too, endorse a narrative of integral solidarity with regard to their national communities in which racial and religious privileges have been handed down from generation to generation. They are part of its tradition. This community exists beyond the liberal rule of law, formal citizenship, or the bureaucratic state. It doesn't require diversity or welfare programs. Members of the community work at their jobs, pray at their churches, participate in their social functions, and support one another in bad times. They grow up together, intermarry, and follow accepted standards of behavior. They also provide the chauvinist with a sense of identity and belonging.

So far as he is concerned, the state is secondary to the community and citizenship is secondary to a kind of experiential participation in its "culture." The bigot thus lives in a prepolitical world. That his culture is the best of all possible cultures is a given. Some variant of "blood and soil" has been an ideological prop for all movements in which the bigot has played a major role. Long before there was any talk about what Samuel Huntington termed "the clash of civilizations" (which actually calls for indifference rather than conflict), instinctual belief in the superiority of certain cultural-psychological propensities served to rationalize hypernationalism and war.[43]

All chauvinists insulate themselves from the stranger, the heathen, and the cosmopolitan. Tradition takes on a value in its own right; reciprocity is denied the Other; and there is an inordinate moral emphasis on the family. Women know their place; incest, spousal abuse, and constraints on opportunity vanish. The future is predetermined. The famous Nazi slogan concerning women— "Children, Church, Kitchen" (*Kinder, Kirche, Küche*)—is only an extension of earlier traditional ideas concerning the place of women in society. Chauvinists everywhere deplore marrying outside the ethnic community.

Spike Lee confronted this latter issue in his film *Jungle Fever* (1991), in which a married black professional has a genuine love affair with an Italian working-class girl. Their relationship founders on their profoundly different cultural experiences. But its destruction is helped along by the embedded prejudices of their friends and families. The film ends with a young white man and young black woman in the same community starting to date. That sign of hope separates Spike Lee's film from the pessimistic ending to a very similar love story set in Alsace-Lorraine by Maurice Barrès about a century earlier in which differing "roots" deny the possibility of intermarriage. Maintaining the community—or his image of the community and the way it once was—is a primary responsibility of the chauvinist. When it comes to critics of the community, the choice is simple: "love it or leave it."

Today, indeed, that slogan has a different connotation than in times past, when it was directed against opponents of the Vietnam War. But the basic message remains. It is *our* community, not theirs. This organic community looked different outside the United States. It was more hierarchical and complex in the rights and duties demanded of its members. Its immutable structure and the privileges accorded the aristocracy were justified in religious terms through notions like the "divine right of kings" and a host of prayers like "God bless our lords and masters and keep us in our proper places." Hatred of Arabs has now overtaken all other prejudices in Europe. But the supposed killing of Jesus by the Jews and their reported preternatural capitalist inclinations served the bigot well in painting them as agents of modernity and enemies of the premodern community. A feudal tradition is obviously lacking in the United States. Nevertheless, the American chauvinist exhibits roughly the same forms of moral cognition as his counterpart elsewhere.

Anti-Semitism was never as virulent in the United States as in Europe. American chauvinists never embraced the notion of hierarchical status based on birth in the manner of other nations. They instead focused on race and the color line and (mostly) a nostalgic view of capitalism based on neighborly, stout, and kind-hearted white individuals "willing to work" together within an essentially homogenous community that reserved a special place for people of color. That the Other doesn't fit in is not the fault of white people. Things are the way they are: the outsider will always be an outsider. Selective memories of stories, experiences, and everyday life confirm the chauvinist's prereflective prejudice. More than the true believer or the elitist, the chauvinist relies on public opinion. Reactionary populism provides him with a unique sense of belonging from which his sense of superiority derives. His public is the only public worth considering so far as the chauvinist is concerned. The cultural life and political grievances of the subaltern play no role. The Other is denied a voice. The bigot doesn't know him—or more importantly, care to know him.

Chauvinists always had their problems with those who tested (and resisted) the moral claims of community. Autonomy frightens them.[44] They feared the Enlightenment with its attack on tradition, religious authority, and the unaccountable and arbitrary exercise of power. Progress is for them one long exercise in alienation and disorientation. The chauvinist is parochial in his view of the world. He cannot understand what is happening to his ethnic ties, his small town in a rural setting, or his comfortable suburb once removed from the ghetto. Thus the chauvinist lacks the proselytizing certitude of the true believer and the cynical self-referential arrogance of the elitist.

Chauvinists envision a past community in which incomes were roughly equal, racial or ethnic homogeneity was a given, religion was respected, and a social hierarchy born of tradition was in place. Limited possibilities for social interaction with the Other militate against a cosmopolitan outlook. The community is composed of friends, unlike the modern public sphere, which is composed of strangers.[45] Blacks doff their hats to whites in the street; you can trust your neighbor; everyone works for a living; and there are no immigrants (or, better, there are only our kind of immigrants). But that community—and by extension the chauvinist himself—is now under attack by cultural diversity, globalization, mass media, secularism, new social movements, and a bureaucratic welfare state.

The chauvinist seems shocked by all this and his narrative must incorporate a response. He wants something to hold onto. In Europe, it is the romantic idea of an autarkic community infused with an integral nationalism that produces what it requires and (in pseudo-socialist fashion) meets the (minimal) economic needs of its members.[46] The alternative response to capitalist development (currently in vogue in the United States) rests on nostalgia for its supposed classical liberal origins in the small town with a free market. Both versions rest on traditional hierarchies, an organic and homogenous understanding of community, and contempt for the Other or the outsider. Both also basically understand the economy in terms of a household. Obsessions with saving, so characteristic of the small businessman, are thus extended to the modern, complex, and institutionally driven economy and the supposedly wasteful interventions of the state.[47]

American chauvinists imagine their ideal community as the small town depicted by television sit-coms like *Father Knows Best, The Andy Griffith Show, Leave It to Beaver,* or *Happy Days*. Liberal ideals are present, but they are given a deeply anachronistic (and reactionary) twist. Citizens are all making a decent living; sheriffs run jails in which there are no prisoners (other than a friendly drunk or two); the nuclear family is fetishized and each has a male breadwinner; education is not really a priority; young people deal with the problems of dating and fitting in; sex awaits marriage; and it's assumed that everyone goes to church (without it being an issue). Life is comfortable: Horatio Alger does not get outrageously rich but instead becomes "respectable." The chauvinist lives in the classical liberal world of a watchman state content to enforce contracts and the basic values associated with the rule of law. The Other never appears: there are no gays, feminists, or people of color (other than in demeaning or subordinate roles). There is also no politics in this imagined community (or the television shows that reflect it), perhaps because, ultimately, there is nothing much to debate. Small-town life was actually marked less by cooperation and the sunny world ideal of the town meeting than by the anti-intellectual, gossipy, stifling, parochial reality depicted in Sinclair Lewis's *Main Street* (1920). But that doesn't interest the bigot. He wants a world in which he feels at home.

Unable or unwilling to interpret the erosion of the organic community as a necessary product of capitalism and its commodity form, yet aware that this erosion is taking place, the chauvinist must seek an answer elsewhere if he is to maintain his identity and existential sense of worth. Freud already noted how narcissism is expressed in the antipathies and aversions that people feel toward the "stranger" who is unlike them.[48] Stereotypical images of the stranger, the outcast, and the refugee reach far back in time. His similarity with the original idea of the scapegoat is eerie. From the first, the stranger was understood as the "ancient figure of the outcast, a man cursed by the gods, an exile who does not deserve a better fate" and since he fits neither in his original nor his new home, an "ideal model for irreconcilability." Hatred of the outcast, indeed, is a way of expressing hatred for the wider world and the "rejection of one's inner potential for freedom."[49]

The stranger poses a danger to the chauvinist's self-serving historical narrative that provides what Gordon Allport termed his "island of safety." On his island, the chauvinist doesn't need to justify his privileges or his prejudices.

He can appear as the good old boy or the patriot or the benevolent master of his domain. But the stranger threatens to destroy all his illusions. The image of "mammy" is a case in point. She is now more or less forgotten, but old songs and novels and movies made reference to her all the time. No need to list the actresses like Butterfly McQueen or Ethel Waters, once a preeminent jazz singer, who played the part. Mammy is ubiquitous and, as the white person sings Irving Caesar's lyrics to George Gershwin's classic "Swanee" (1919), she is always "waitin' for me, prayin' for me, down by the Swanee." Following the Civil War, of course, the defeated South witnessed the rise of the Ku Klux Klan along with the lynching of blacks, arson against blacks, trumped-up trials of blacks, campaigns against their attempts to secure basic rights, and the branding of blacks as an alien community. Under the circumstances, indeed, it is worth considering whether the chauvinist (and his modern admirers) actually believed that these "mammies" were quite so preoccupied with the happiness of their privileged white charges.

On April 10, 2012, the 150th anniversary of the beginning of the Civil War, CNN released a poll showing that 25 percent of the general public and 40 percent of Southerners sympathize more with the Confederacy than with the Union. With the blessing of the Republican-dominated city council in Selma, Alabama, a legendary site for the

Civil Rights Movement, ground was broken in 2012 for a monument dedicated to the Confederate general Nathan Bedford Forrest, who was the first grand wizard of the KKK and who slaughtered black Union soldiers at the battle of Fort Pillow during the Civil War. More than half of Republicans surveyed also believe that slavery was *not* the cause of the conflict; it was really about states' rights, not about race. It was a war between Americans—or, better, white Americans—and, so it logically follows, their traditions deserve to be celebrated by Americans today. As mentioned earlier, chauvinists from that part of the country still like to claim that "it's about heritage, not about race."

So let's cut to the less distant past: December 20, 2010, was "shaping up to be quite a night in Charleston. Confederate enthusiasts [were] throwing a grand ball there to celebrate the 150th anniversary of the state's secession from the Union. Hundreds of people, many decked out in hoop skirts and militia uniforms, [would] drink mint juleps and dance the night away."[50] Organizers of the event insisted that it had nothing to do with slavery or racism; NAACP activists protesting the event seemed to disagree. The activists recalled the huge demonstrations of former slaves that had celebrated the end of slavery and the fall of Charleston to Union forces in 1865. But that didn't matter very much to the revelers. For the chauvinists who were determined to promote their version of history, protests in the present, like the celebrations in the past, were the work of those who were never really part of the community in the first place. Like all other bigots, the chauvinist believes that his victim only has himself to blame for his woes.

The chauvinist's knowledge of the Other, born of his prejudice, is what Martin Heidegger would term "ready at hand." Whether generated in rural areas or the suburbs, it is a reflex reaction against a changing world that bolsters the chauvinist's self-image. Like the true believer and the elitist, the chauvinist is completely self-absorbed. His vision of an organic community and some "golden age" empowers him. The best is what was—because what was privileged him. The chauvinist senses that "where everything aims to view the future and its possibilities in terms of the past, where expectations can be only variations on what already exists or what did exist, progressive forces of humanity are in constant danger of atrophy."[51] The chauvinist intuits that they are on the march. Little wonder that our polarized politics should rest on a growing divide between the white Christian male and an increasingly hybrid secular constituency intent on contesting his privileges and his prejudices.

Experience of the Other is probably the best way to combat bigotry. But the chauvinist is shy—and, besides, he cannot bear the gaze of his victim. It is immaterial whether that gaze is being directed at him by Native Americans who obviously should have celebrated Manifest Destiny, Latin Americans whose safety has supposedly been preserved by the Monroe Doctrine, African Americans, women, or those in the previously colonized world saved from communism. What counts is that the bigot is being seen negatively and that his knowledge of events, his perspective on himself, is being challenged. Multicultural education and revisionist history question his hegemony. They also contradict what "everyone" knows and that, in turn, only makes the chauvinist more resentful. Like a child, he wants the story told the same way over and over and over again. He has no use for counter-narratives or revisionist history. His arguments are not meant to foster either critical analysis or debate. That would only complicate matters and, from the bigot's standpoint—the subaltern and her allies have made things complicated enough.

The bigot has no use for pluralism, but it is a different matter with respect to relativism. Lending itself easily to projection, relativism is also a convenient legitimating device. The Hindu cannot criticize the Islamic bigot for persecuting Hindus since Hindu bigots have long persecuted Muslims. Germans condemned by Americans in the aftermath of World War II for murdering Jews often pointed to the lynching of blacks in the South to mitigate their own guilt.[52] Relativism defines the discourse. The chauvinist searches for excuses and selects his material accordingly. He knows what he wants taught and he wants it taught in the fashion that suits him—and only him.

Alfred Rosenberg, the court philosopher of Hitler, made this clear with his famous statement: "Right is what Aryan men hold to be right." Normative judgments cannot be introduced by those outside the community. Insiders always have a deeper experiential knowledge than the outsider. That the bigot's interpretation of the past never seems to fit with that of his victim is obviously due to the innate intelligence of the bigot and the innate stupidity of his chosen target. The subaltern has never appreciated the bigot's wisdom. This frustrates him and the extent to which it does is the extent to which his recourse to violence is justified: the unappreciated Other must be made appreciative and forced to learn. The chauvinist does not believe that "the community is a choice of belonging and not a cultural heritage."[53] The bigoted heritage of the past is what gives the chauvinist his power. The community provides a feeling of solidarity and this feeling shapes his understanding of tradition. The bigot alone will decide on the views of the founders, the meaning of the constitution, and what it means to live in the shining city on the hill.

FOUR

The Bigot Today

James Baldwin once wrote that the authors of destruction want innocence.[1] The bigot's roles provide that. They provide the bigot with legitimacy as he practices his craft today. Burdened with the legacy of Auschwitz, scarred by anti-imperialist movements, chastened by the Civil Rights Movement and its heirs, he camouflages his intentions in order to function in an ever more complex global society. The white hoods and swastikas now exist only at the margins. The bigot often recoils when accused of prejudice. His racist and sexist statements are made but then withdrawn; his inferences are provided and then amended; his biased claims are argued and then qualified. The old-fashioned rhetoric now provides only background noise. Racism is no longer embedded in the academic curriculum;

bigotry lacks a new literature; and, in spite of Fox News, reactionary attitudes run counter to the liberal demands of the mass media. All minorities in liberal democracies have their lobbies and interest groups: hate crimes are prosecuted, synagogues are given state protection, and there are frequent attempts to mediate residual tensions. The bigot feels the influence of this shift in the public discourse. He now appears as the respectable protector of society from cultural pluralists, "welfare cheats," and those who want something for nothing. He even claims to have become color blind as he attempts to reclaim "traditional America" and its increasingly imperiled liberty. Nevertheless, the bigot still tends toward the more radical and reactionary end of the conservative spectrum.

The bigot senses that what Walter Benjamin termed the "aura" of divine experience has been ripped away.[2] Few people today possess the kind of everyday theological knowledge that once was common; the organic society in which religious tradition flourished is a thing of the past. The old integrated system of beliefs and rituals is becoming a buffet from which each individual can choose what he likes and ignore what inconveniences him. Most Catholics today have used some form of contraception; most Jews do not keep a kosher household; and most Muslims do not pray five times a day. Personal experience is now tainted by technological production; commercial media are the source of knowledge; and the encounter with the alien, the blasphemer, the heretic—the Other—is inscribed in an increasingly cosmopolitan context. Technology and tradition now reinforce one another. The bigot is both fascinated and appalled by the culture industry, consumerism, and radical individualism. Thus he builds a "mega-church," and employs mass media and shock radio, the Internet, lobbyists, and huge textbook markets to challenge critical narratives about the imperialist, racist, and exploitative elements of American history.

Caught within a Manichean universe of his own construction, the bigot understands politics as a zero-sum game. He feels he is losing power to the degree that the subaltern is gaining it. This allows him to hide behind the "conservative" label. Wearing the garb of the true believer, the elitist, and the chauvinist, his prejudice insinuates itself into seemingly mainstream policy discussions. While the bigot anticipates translating his visions of a mythical community into legislation, the opportunistic conservative knows who can provide him with support. Both view the failings of modern society as having less to do with its exclusionary and exploitative traditions, or its arbitrary exercises of political and economic power, than the subaltern's strivings to change them. The bigot's cluster of targets is no different than that of the more traditional conservative: those comprising the various new social movements and the new multicultural working class. Yet it is the bigot and his genuinely reactionary comrades who mobilize the masses while the establishmentarian with his conservative disposition tends to join later.

Both the bigot and the conservative ignore the continuing institutional and symbolic prejudice against gays, immigrants, women, and people of color. They know what groups benefit most from the welfare state and pro-labor legislation. They can imagine what gay marriage would mean not only for the gay community, but also for liberal democracy. They understand what "self-deportation" and restrictions on social services imply for immigrants. They can envision the effects on women in general and poor women in particular of withdrawing governmental support for organizations like Planned Parenthood, research into breast and cervical cancer, prenatal and day care, free contraception, and abortion rights. They surely know that convicts can't vote and that privatizing the prison system, which has put more than 2.3 million people behind bars, 70 percent of whom are people of color, has created what has legitimately been called the "new Jim Crow."[3]

More acceptable language veils the reality—though the old rhetoric occasionally still breaks through. Ultimately, however, it is the practice of prejudice that identifies the bigot today. Traditional racial stereotypes may still blend with talk of individual responsibility and initiative. Explanation of broader economic trends is still left to the racist imagination and conspiracy fetishism. Attacks on "socialist" programs and "entitlements" targeting minorities still mix with attempts to constrict democracy. The bigot's newly packaged politics of resentment shifts the conservative discourse to the right. But his use of camouflage makes it more difficult to focus on the practice of prejudice and his attempts to reduce the subaltern to the predetermined Other. It is easy to be misled. Nevertheless, there is little justification in speaking blithely about the "end" of racism or the disappearance of bigotry.

More than ten thousand hate websites currently exist, and their crude (often pseudo-scholarly) articles are directed primarily to young people and even preteens. Fears of the stranger remain. Scapegoats are still easy to find. Old habits die hard. Congo, Darfur, and Rwanda serve as reminders of genocidal tribal and ethnic hatred. A woman was beheaded for witchcraft in Saudi Arabia in 2011; hundreds watched as seven Israeli teenagers attempted to lynch some Palestinian youths in Jerusalem in 2012.[4] With the connivance of the police, six German citizens of Turkish and Greek extraction (along with a policewoman) were victims of the "Doener murders" carried out by the National Socialist Underground between 2000 and 2007. Sex trafficking has become an international addiction. Everywhere there is an outcry on the right against immigrants, and many mainstream conservative leaders insist that the multicultural state has failed. A study released in December 2011 by the UN High Commissioner for Human Rights reported that seventy-six countries criminalize homosexuality and that gay and transgender people not only risk the death penalty in five nations, but also are subject to organized discrimination and street violence with a "high degree of cruelty" in all regions of the world.[5]

European bigots have targeted (especially) Roma and Arab immigrants in the name of maintaining the continent's (white Christian) European identity and liberal values. Using this form of camouflage, the Progress Party of Norway won 23 percent of the vote in 2009, Geert Wilders Party for Freedom received 15.5 percent in the Danish elections of 2010, the ultra-right-wing Sweden Democrats entered parliament with nearly 6 percent, the True Finns won 19 percent, and the arch-reactionary National Front of Marine Le Pen took 18 percent of the French vote in 2012.[6] Amid fears of economic collapse in 2012–2013, the Greek neo-fascist party "Golden Dawn" has drawn attention by physically attacking immigrants in the streets, engaging in pitched battles with "communists," and expanding its enemies list to include "subversive" feminists, gays, and prominent secular intellectuals.[7] In Europe, too, there is much grumbling about the decline of traditional morality, miscegenation, and a growing welfare state that is seemingly granting ever greater benefits to ever larger nonwhite immigrant communities.

Integral nationalism, anti-democratic elitism, and reliance on religious authority still intoxicate the true believer, the elitist, the chauvinist, and—too often—even the establishmentarian conservative. All of them understand that constitutionalism and suffrage reject—in principle—the idea of individuals living in a community without explicit and guaranteed civil liberties, bound together only by land and custom. They know that liberal democracy assumes a social contract that projects a universal notion of the citizen and limits on the arbitrary exercise of power.

Such ideals did not instantly translate into reality. Anti-Semitism, patriarchy, racism, religious intolerance, and slavery still continued to exist during the age of democratic revolution. Men without property were denied the vote. Citizenship was initially restricted to a tiny minority. Attempts to identify humanity with white men—and universal precepts with their interests—were eventually challenged by women, slaves, workers, and the rest of the disenfranchised and exploited. Conservatives and bigots tended to ally in contesting those efforts. Worth noting is that the failure to implement full political and social equality among citizens was due less to the inadequacies of progressives than the obstacles created by reactionaries who now so often congratulate themselves on their flexibility.

Neither bigots nor conservatives were ever comfortable with liberals and socialists (albeit not always to the same degree), and they have generally been unable to distinguish between them. They didn't particularly like each other either. But when forced to choose between left and right, it usually didn't take either of them long to decide. The liberal rule of law is antithetical to the prejudices of the bigot while the ideal of economic equality empowers the subaltern whom he hates. That liberals and socialists played such an important role in the anti-fascist struggle only made the bigot's situation more difficult later. Liberal ideals and individual dignity gained new standing in the aftermath of World War II. The Civil Rights Movement led by Dr. Martin Luther King, Jr., initiated what soon became a broader challenge to racist, patriarchal, and homophobic prejudices that were ingrained in the mainstream understanding of how society should be organized and what the character of the national community should be. Political participation grew, sexual relations became less rigid, new experiences were sought, new welfare policies were enacted with the "great society" programs of President Lyndon Johnson, cultural identities multiplied, and a new sympathy emerged for the Other. Europe experienced a call by young people to confront its fascist legacy by "working through the past."

Anxious over his looming identity deficit, insecure over

his diminished status, feeling unwanted and unappreciated, the bigot was thrown on the defensive. He sought a
degree of respectability by embracing notions like "human
rights" and "social justice" and then identifying them with
the special privileges to which he still feels entitled and
the imperiled liberty of powerful institutions under attack
from below. In the United States, "Dixiecrats," fearing the
abolition of segregation, threatened to split the Democratic Party in 1948. Ultimately, passage in 1964 of the
Civil Rights Act and in 1965 of the Voting Rights Act led
the Southern states to abandon their traditional support
of the Democratic Party and switch to the Republicans.
The bigot changed parties but the true believer, the elitist,
and the chauvinist still wound up with the same traditional
constituencies. They came in the form of the burgeoning
evangelical movement and the moral majority, supporters
of "trickle down" economics and an assault on the welfare
state, as well as those preoccupied with black-on-white
crime and the champions of hypernationalism. Speakers
at the Republican Convention of 1992 warned that a "culture war" was taking place in the United States with liberals and radical remnants of the 1960s supporting abortion,
feminism, "homosexual rights," and what Norman Podhoretz derisively termed "the adversary culture."[8]

Free markets, militarism, and parochialism blended in
the neoconservative ideology that marked the presidency

of George W. Bush (2000–2008). In the aftermath of 9/11, bewildered and caught unaware, the chauvinist and his allies started projecting American anxieties on an "axis of evil" initially composed of Iran, Iraq, and North Korea. At the same time, however, the United States was coddling Saudi Arabia along with a host of brutal secular dictators ruling other Middle Eastern states. In this way, the global impression of a double standard at work was heightened. The situation only grew worse as preemptive strikes were undertaken against Afghanistan and Iraq. Orientalism with its stereotypic images of Arabs helped set the stage for this new foreign policy and the emergence of a national security state.[9] Under the watch of President Bush, welfare programs were curtailed, government regulations on business were loosened, and the greatest upward shift in wealth in American history took place.[10]

Camouflage was easy to create and the true believer, the elitist, and the chauvinist seemed to fit in perfectly with the (neo)conservative mainstream. Following the economic collapse of 2008, and the election of a black president, the Tea Party energized the prejudices of a reactionary mass base for what became an increasingly bitter class offensive. More and more, it became a matter of "us" against "them." The Tea Party legitimized forms of intolerance that many believed had lost their appeal. Its members applauded as a few lunatic pastors threatened to burn the Koran and condemned Islam as a religion of the "gutter." Old stereotypes about African Americans, gays, Latinos, and women resurfaced with a vengeance. These were reinforced by an anti-intellectual, anti-scientific, and paranoid cultural outlook that dismissed global warming and climate change as hoaxes perpetrated by a conspiracy among scientists intent on curtailing consumption and weakening American industry.

Establishmentarian conservatism soon gave comfort to the bigot. Adherents shared with bigots an opposition to government regulation, unions, immigrants, taxes, affirmative action, voting rights, secularism, the welfare state and cultural pluralism. Conservatives will, of course, deny any suggestion of bigotry, but their hodge-podge of positions in the second decade of the twenty-first century cannot be explained any other way. There is no inherent reason why economic libertarianism should align with religious conservatism. There is also no inherent reason why a belief in open markets should align with opposition to immigration or constriction of voting rights. But that is now the case. Each of these alliances adds grist to the bigot's mill. After embracing the Tea Party, Republicans moved to the right. Intolerance became fashionable. The bigot became integrated into the conservative mainstream. His camouflaged prejudice was legitimated and perhaps he was no longer even aware of his bigotry. Hypocrisy blended with belief, opportunism with conviction. But the bigot remained who he was. With his religious dogmatism, his anti-democratic elitism, and his parochial understanding of community, he still exemplifies the underside of the revolutionary struggle for cosmopolitanism, political liberty, and social equality.

Freedom has never been a problem for the bigot because he already possesses it. The "problem" arises only when freedom is demanded by the disenfranchised, the exploited, and the excluded. The attack on the welfare state is actually an attack on public welfare. But ideology is not a simple reflex of economic interest. The bigot is often willing to grit his teeth, take the moral high ground, and reject policies that might actually serve his material interests. Deep in his heart he may also want any number of government programs, but forgoing them is worth it—so long as the Other doesn't benefit.

Existential interests often take precedence over material ones. The bigot's political positions are fortified by his inability to understand how the economic system works. Talk of cultural decay and national deracination leave no room for discussions of capital flight, deskilling, cuts in education and job-training programs, institutional racism, and conflicts deriving from existing structural imbalances of power. The bigot lacks categories for meaningfully interpreting modernity. He feels that lack. Thus the true believer looks upward; the elitist talks unctuously about self-help; the chauvinist sighs; and the fanatic seethes.

Tea Time

American politics is generally seen as nonideological and pragmatic. Sometimes driven to the left, other times to the right, the pendulum always seems to swing back to what the liberal historian Arthur Schlesinger termed the "vital center."[11] But right-wing extremism has actually been a constant. American political institutions may minimize the prospects of ideologically driven political parties seizing state power, but scores of reactionary mass movements have pressured the electoral process and tainted the cultural atmosphere since the nation's founding. The bigot has always felt at home in the United States. He was welcomed by the "Know-Nothings" of the 1840s, the Ku Klux Klan, the mostly forgotten yet powerful "America First" movement that preferred Hitler to FDR, the partisans of Joseph McCarthy, the "Dixiecrat" constituency that served as the Southern wing of the Democratic Party from the end of the Civil War until 1964, the John Birch Society, as well as the "silent" majority of the 1960s and the "moral" majority of the 1980s. All have had their true believers, elitists, and chauvinists, and all of them defended economic inequality as well as an idealized vision of the American past. This tradition of theory and practice, which is less establishmentarian conservative than radical reactionary, has provided deep-seated networks of meaning and signification for the contemporary bigot and the Tea Party.[12]

With a membership of roughly two hundred thousand, organized locally in about a thousand relatively small groups spanning the country, the Tea Party enjoys "strong" support from about 20 percent of the voting populace, or about 46 million Americans.[13] It received funding and support from reactionary stalwarts like the Koch brothers and former House majority leader Dick Armey's "Freedom-Works" organization. But the Tea Party was not built from the top down. Driven not so much by losers, but by those imperiled by progress, it represents an entrenched constituency fearful of the liberal, egalitarian, pluralistic, secular, and urban elements of modernity.[14] Coming from nonurban communities mostly in the South and the Midwest, but also from white immigrant enclaves in some big cities, those in the Tea Party have their own deeply reactionary forms of moral cognition predicated on the use of traditional myths, stereotypes, and uses of the double standard.

Straddling the social hierarchy between genuine capitalists and workers, its membership is overwhelmingly white, lower middle class, and decidedly nonunion. It also includes many small business owners and independent contractors. Tea Party members are educated but resentful of Ivy League types, urban life, and the cosmopolitan dynamics of modernity. Lacking the cultural and social capital of the upwardly mobile professional strata, whose style and privileges they disdain, their incomes are mostly above the national average. Members of the Tea Party are pessimistic when it comes to the future—economically, culturally, and politically. Wearing revolutionary garb and tricorn hats, disrupting town meetings devoted to health care and other social issues, bullying progressive congressional representatives and holding rallies of their own, they compensate for their identity deficit by calling for "revolution"—though, naturally, one that will protect their privileges and interests.

Why must the little guy—or, better, the white guy— always pay the taxes, shoulder the burden, and get the shaft? The bigot endorses the Tea Party's attempt to mesh libertarian capitalism with a parochial populism preoccupied with family values, religion, and a mythical vision of community. Over the last century, for the most part, these trends were diametrically at odds with one another: libertarians had little use for rabble-rousing chauvinists, religious fanatics, or small-minded elitists, while populists hated big business, open markets, and the scientific culture of modernity. But there was new urgency for an organizational alliance between them following the economic collapse and subsequent presidential victory of Barack Obama in 2008. Fears of dramatic state intervention into the economy blended with concerns over the symbolism of having a cultivated black president lead an America that is becoming so multicultural that by 2020 white people (and particularly white men) will no longer be in the majority.

Out of this alliance and these anxieties the Tea Party was born in 2009. Without a vision, still reeling from its defeat in the presidential elections, the GOP felt itself overwhelmed by what many professionals previously considered fringe elements of the far right. The party's mass base was infuriated by bank bailouts, healthcare legislation, an explosion of state programs, and—of course—a black president. The new president was seen as "anti-American" and an advocate for (black) welfare "cheats," (Latino) immigrant "criminals," as well as anti-Christian (Arab) "terrorist" and "anti-family" (feminist and gay) forces. The Tea Party channeled the bigot's prejudices. At the same time, for him, identifying with big business and its (seemingly) color-blind attack on the welfare state seemed necessary for recreating a patriarchal world of white privilege.

Moderate Republicans found themselves isolated. Their political party no longer appeared to welcome pragmatic conservatives cut in the mold of General Colin Powell or

Senators Chuck Hagel (Nebraska), Richard Luger (Indiana), or Olympia Snowe (Maine). New reactionary politicians indebted to the Tea Party now refused to compromise with the Democrats on vote after vote: healthcare, unemployment benefits, student loans, tax cuts for the wealthy, and a host of other bills. The spotlight was increasingly cast on religious dogmatists, intolerant elitists, and homespun chauvinists. Seasoned operatives of the Republican Party were unable to forge a general consensus as they nervously offered their advice and leadership. Mainstream conservatives initially thought the Tea Party might be manipulated. But the tail wound up wagging the dog.

With the sweeping victory of the far right in the Congressional elections of 2010, the Tea Party's agenda spilled over into that of the Republican Party: its ideology blended with that of the conservative mainstream.[15] Not only the Tea Party but also the Republican Party directly challenged the legacy of the New Deal, and conservatives embraced capitalist fundamentalism. Right-wing activists now considered the "invisible hand" of the market and the individual (not the accumulation process and class) as the primary elements of economic analysis. In line with the visions of their imaginary community, they came to understand government spending in terms of a household budget. Individuals, they insisted, are only responsible for themselves. The welfare state and its redistributive economic programs were condemned not merely as wasteful—but also as immoral. Former senator Rick Santorum (R-Pennsylvania)—a darling of the Tea Party—noted that "there is income inequality in America. There always has been and, hopefully, and I do say that, there always will be."[16]

Many members of the Tea Party may (secretly) support Social Security, healthcare, and the like.[17] But they seem willing to forgo their benefits so long as women, people of color, immigrants, and gays are also deprived of them. Contempt for the Other trumps material interest. With the growing influence of the Tea Party, the once modest home afforded the bigot by the Republican Party turned into a mansion. Still, he now appears willing to embrace supposed representatives of the subaltern so long as they function something like the "court Jew" of times past. Former vice presidential candidate Sarah Palin (R-Alaska) and former congresswoman Michele Bachmann (R-Minnesota) reaffirmed the image of a stay-at-home "hockey mom" in a world where the single breadwinner is becoming an anachronism. Their supporters among right-wing media pundits publicly labeled women advocating the use of contraception as "sluts" and feminists as "bitches," while Tea Party politicians questioned prenatal screening and (without offering a meaningful alternative) opposed the Violence against Women Act. Herman Cain, a businessman and one-time presidential candidate, also made a big splash by insisting that African Americans had been "brain-washed" into supporting the Democratic Party, thereby confirming the bigot's stereotypical belief that they are too stupid to make political choices on their own. Former Congressman Allen West (R-Florida) agreed and, for good measure, identified the Democratic Party with the Nazi propaganda machine.

This colorful cast of characters associated with the Tea Party, it should be noted, was not particularly useful for converting the undecided among the electorate. Their more important function was to reinforce the bigot's idealized image of himself and how a person of color or a woman should behave. They validated the benevolent image of a bygone America in which taxes were low, government was small, and the only important color was white. "Common sense" insulates such people from criticism and the need for further learning. They view themselves as rebels or revolutionaries. Feeling betrayed by moderate conservatives, intuitively understanding that modernity is the enemy, the Tea Party wants a simpler world in which traditional privileges go unchallenged and in which (as the old joke goes) "men are men and women are glad of it." In this mythical world, people marry their own kind; homosexuals stay in the closet; and immigrants and people of color know their place.

The 2012 platform of the Texas Republican Party, for

example, called for repealing the Voting Rights Act of 1965, opposing the "morning after" pill, condemning homosexuality, withdrawing from the United Nations, supporting "traditional" marriage; affirming Judeo-Christian values, withholding Supreme Court jurisdiction in cases involving abortion, religious freedom, and the Bill of Rights—and, just to be safe, making sure that Sharia law won't be enacted. As for the national GOP, there is hardly a single policy proposal that does not disadvantage gays, people of color, women, and working people—and, worse, there was hardly a single major Republican politician willing to challenge the radical right's agenda in the primaries of 2012. All candidates for the Republican presidential nomination worried publicly about a "disappearing white majority." Close to half of Republican voters in Mississippi still support banning interracial marriage and gay marriage. Attitudes are not that different elsewhere in the Deep South. Little wonder that twenty states had petitions seeking secession from the United States following the presidential election of 2012.

Approving winks by the mainstream are given all the time. Terms like "tar baby," "slut," and "fag," as well as positive references to the Confederacy, may be frowned on in public, but they are frequently whispered by mainstream conservatives in private. The influence of words on action may be indirect, but it is still palpable. Everyday

violence (that mostly goes unreported) against homosexuals, immigrants, and minorities remains a routine
fact of American life. Doctors performing abortions outside the larger cities now do so at their own risk. White
supremacists of varying shades mix with Republicans and
luminaries of the Tea Party at various conferences like
those hosted by the American Conservative Union in 2011.
It is a mistake to think that explicit calls for violence come
only from the margins. Ann Coulter called for poisoning
a Supreme Court justice; certain elected officials in Texas
warned of insurrection were President Obama to be re-
elected; and Sarah Palin's website showed gun sights
trained on the nearly assassinated Congresswoman Gabrielle Giffords (D-Arizona).[18] Sometimes it is hard to
tell when violent language crosses the line from the meta-
phorical to the literal, but clearly the Tea Party has given
new hope to reactionary fanatics. In spite of all the political assassinations that have marked American history, and
the numerous terrible massacres of young people and
children at primary and high schools, it's safe to say that
the near obsession of Tea Party members with the right
to own firearms (including the AK-47) does not merely
express their desire to hunt ducks.

Mainstream politicians of the Republican Party fell into
line.[19] They feared being labeled a "RINO" ("Republican
in name only"). Mitt Romney won his party's presidential

nomination in 2012 by vacillating between defending the moderate conservatism of his political past and pandering to his party's radically right-wing base. Republicans promised to "starve the beast" that they identified with the welfare state, oppose "Obamacare," turn Social Security and Medicare into voucher programs, maintain tax inequities that favor the top 2 percent, deregulate markets, and abolish various governmental agencies. They also opposed gay rights and gay marriage, funding women's health organizations and the right to abortion, as well as "critical thinking" in education, evolution, a multicultural historical narrative, and maintaining the "wall of separation" between church and state. In addition, Republicans supported eliminating limits on campaign spending and voting restrictions that would effectively disenfranchise hundreds of thousands of citizens and especially poor people of color.

Conservative commentators and right-wing political experts were amazed, however, when Romney lost the election with 47.6 percent of the vote (versus 50.7 percent for President Obama). This was only slightly more than the 45.6 percent who voted for Senator John McCain and Governor Sarah Palin (against 52.9 percent for Obama) in 2008, when Republicans were saddled with blame for two failed wars, the bursting of the subprime housing bubble, the crashing of the derivates market, and perhaps the weakest presidential ticket in recent memory.

But the most prominent explanations for the Republican defeat never called into question their attack on the Other, or their use of the double standard, projection, elitism, chauvinism, stereotypes, true belief, paranoia, and conspiracy fetishism. Mitt Romney insisted that while Republicans offered scores of policies beneficial to big business, the Democrats won by giving welfare "gifts" to their ("entitled") constituencies of immigrants, people of color, women, and workers; Karl Rove suggested that the Democrats had suppressed the vote; Dick Morris insisted that Republicans would win in a "landslide" and afterward noted sagely that they lost because of "demographic mathematics"; and Ann Coulter blamed "stupid single women" for the Obama victory while adding, for good measure, that "women shouldn't vote" and that the Democratic Party should be "hanging its head in shame" at its inability to attract white men.[20] Bill O'Reilly claimed that 2012 constituted the defeat of "traditional America"; right-wing preachers wailed about moral decline and creeping secularism; while close to half of the Republican Party apparently reached the conclusion that ACORN, a small radical activist group that no longer exists, "stole" the election for Obama.[21]

Old prejudices underpin this cluster of claims. There is a sense here that liberals and their supporters among gays, people of color, and women have no concept or regard for governance. They vote only for politicians willing to re-distribute wealth and transfer government resources into their hands. These groups are seemingly always ready to be bribed. They lack a moral core and a sense of what is right, wisdom and a larger perspective, patriotism, and an understanding of the proper role of government. Finally, those who oppose this giveaway of what O'Reilly called "stuff"—the viewers whom O'Reilly was presumably addressing on Fox—stand on the opposite side of this description. They do not want government handouts. They consider themselves honest, hardworking people with traditional values who know what America is about. They pay their taxes that translate into the benefits that Obama is giving away to the Other. Indeed, "makers versus takers" is not a concept that is overtly prejudiced, but it is surely comforting to the bigot because the underlying assumptions are deeply prejudicial. Is it really the case that only the majority of "angry white men," the only constituency that voted Republican, is capable of making honorable electoral decisions?

All of this is serious business and not only for the loser who cannot make sense of what he has lost or why he has lost it. Perhaps the Tea Party as an organization will find itself in the trashcan of history once Republicans suffer more electoral defeats. New battles will surely occur between moderate conservatives and right-wing extremists in their ranks over economic and other issues, such as how to deal with gay marriage, Social Security, or a growing Latino population. But the arch-reactionary agenda inspired by paranoia, intolerance, and misplaced nostalgia still received electoral support from nearly half of American voters in 2012. In spite of demographic changes, which will leave white people in the minority, the bigot will survive. In fact, his increasingly imperiled status will probably make his mass base all the more intransigent. New organizational forms that meet the needs of this entrenched constituency will undoubtedly emerge in the future as they always have in the past. The bigot can breathe a sigh of relief. He has no need to worry.

Resistance

A new critical public philosophy is required for dealing with the bigot today. Such an enterprise rests on bringing him out of the shadows and then reversing the cultural, political, and economic endeavors in which he is engaged. It remains necessary to deconstruct his discourse and reassert an understanding of the Other as an exploited and disenfranchised person intent on changing his condition. This involves clarifying the prejudices and privileges masked in policy debates so that everyday people can evaluate them appropriately.[22] It also means holding those who disadvantage the subaltern and serve the bigot's interests morally accountable. Too much hand-wringing has taken place over whether this or that person (usually a celebrity) is *really* a bigot deep in his heart. There has been a bit too much parsing of language and examination of attitudes, and not enough critical investigation of political policies.

Everyday citizens become incensed when some commentator lets slip a racist or politically incorrect phrase. But they are far less outraged when confronted with policies that blatantly disadvantage the bigot's traditional targets: gays, immigrants, people of color, and women. Of course, reasonable people can disagree on this or that issue or policy and whether it does indeed advantage the disadvantaged. But when a legislative pattern emerges that lacks any significant support among disadvantaged groups it is another story entirely. Diverse pieces of legislation then congeal into an agenda of bigotry whether its authors are conscious of this or not. Prejudice is not simply a matter of what people say that they feel but how they act and what political positions they take. Confronting the bigot today requires a more explicit emphasis on class, a more cosmopolitan sensibility, and a more robust defense of political liberalism.

Unfortunately, popular understandings of the bigot remain anchored in an earlier time. They fasten on the personal rather than the political, vile language and sensational acts rather than mundane legislation and complicated policy decisions. Many are unwilling to admit that prejudice has entered the mainstream with new justifications. They find it easier to associate prejudice with certain attitudes supposedly on the fringes of public life. But this avoids the ways in which the bigot now employs camouflage in translating his prejudices into reality. To forestall criticism, he now makes use of supposedly "color-blind" economic and anti-crime policies, liberal notions of tolerance, individualism, the entrepreneurial spirit, local government, historical traditions, patriotism, and fears of virtually nonexistent voter fraud to maintain the integrity of the electoral process. Prejudice still appears in clusters, and the bigot's identity deficit is growing larger. Nevertheless, today he is often unaware either that he has prejudices or that he is indulging them.

Contesting bigotry without spawning new forms of it has always been the test of progressive politics. Defense of civil rights and reciprocity under the liberal rule of law is (and remains) the first step in that process. Common civility is the second. It counteracts the vulgarity, intolerance, arrogance, and hatred that mark the bigot. That the demand for civility in public life is considered almost

quaint today attests to the continued existence of circumstances in which the bigot can thrive. Civility makes tolerance concrete: it enables the individual to take the Other
seriously, curb his own arrogance, and learn from those
who are different. There are no fixed criteria to offer when
it comes to civility and politeness—but certainly provoc-
ative chest thumping about identity or the language of
intolerance is the opposite of either.

Civility does not exclude boycotts, protests, and the
use of social opprobrium against the practitioners of prejudice. It is imperative, however, for navigating differences
among the subaltern. Learning to disagree and deal with
the confusions attendant on living in a pluralistic world
is not very different from learning a craft.[23] It requires
educating the sentiments in a way that is antithetical to
bigotry. What Sartre noted in a different context is surely
the case when it comes to the cosmopolitan understanding of personal identity, namely that each is as good as any
but better than none.[24]

Awakening a person's interest with regard to how he is
seen by the Other is an elemental moment of cosmopolitan education. Only in that way can he confront his community's history in a critical fashion. Baldwin once noted
that the reason white people should learn something about
black people is because that is the way in which they can
learn something about themselves. The same kind of think-

ing holds for the Arab and the Jew, the Hindu and the Muslim, and any set of individuals involved in a binary conflict. The point is to spark interest in the Other and the multiple contrasting and often conflicting traditions that comprise her culture. A person who cannot judge between traditions within a group or community is still enmeshed in the world of the stereotype. Not merely schools and universities, but travel and new forms of mass media have a crucial role to play in the process.

The cosmopolitan sensibility has harbored a liberal bias since the Enlightenment and the publication of Immanuel Kant's famous essay "Idea for a Universal History with a Cosmopolitan Purpose" (1784). Worth noting is that the ideals associated with humanity appear in history only if one is willing to look for them. Invoking diversity only contributes to a war of each against all if each subaltern groups aims to justify why its oppression must somehow always take precedence. Solidarity requires a very different sensibility, a kind of curiosity about other cultures and identities as well as a willingness to integrate their contributions into one's own. Genuine respect for the Other presupposes a willingness to engage him and learn about him. This becomes easier insofar as the liberal rule of law is operative and the exercise of individual identity becomes possible. With respect to privileging the passions of this or that constituency, however, the cosmopolitan sensibility assumes not simply tolerance but also what Ian Buruma correctly termed "an informal code of constraint that makes civilized life possible."[25]

The bigot understands constraint in a different way. His aim is to narrow the participation of subaltern groups in society without making reference to his prejudices. Challenging legal activism, an endeavor that had proven so important for the Civil Rights Movement, has today become part of the bigot's more general political attempt to keep the Other in his place. Calling for the abolition of limits on campaign spending and introducing new requirements for voting dovetails with a new legal outlook in which all court decisions would become based on the "original intent" of the Founding Fathers and a "strict construction" of the Constitution.[26] Noteworthy is the way in which the "originalist" interpretation of the Constitution mirrors the true believer's interpretation of the Bible, how the interests of strict constructionists advocated by "originalists" mirror those of the chauvinist, and how the refusal to redress pressing issues of difference and equality is justified by reliance on the supposedly timeless decisions of "great men" and the conservative disposition of elitists. The doctrine evinces little sense of elemental fairness, universality, or what Montesquieu termed "the spirit of the laws."

Originalism works on the assumption that religion,

conservative institutions, free markets, and individualism have been imperiled by the decisions of liberal justices intent on extending the meaning of the Constitution and expanding the power of the courts and the state into everyday life. That its supporters wish to ban abortion through state action speaks to the double standard. But, more generally, "originalism" serves as a vehicle for rolling back the advances made by subaltern groups. In gutting the Voting Rights Act of 1965, for example, the Supreme Court on June 26, 2013, restricted early voting, sanctioned voter identification laws, and allowed for redistricting (presumably according to racial demographics) without federal approval. Staunch advocates of originalism include Supreme Court Justice Antonin Scalia and Robert Bork, whose nomination to the highest court was rejected by the Senate in 1988 perhaps because of his stated opposition to *Brown v. Board of Education*, the Civil Rights Act of 1964, and *Roe v. Wade*. Rather than adapt law to new circumstances, and highlight its critical and historical character, the originalist interpretation presupposes a mythical community in which the privileges and prejudices of white males were taken for granted. It undermines any attempt that seeks, as C. W. Mills put the matter, to transform "private troubles into public issues."[27]

The bigot wishes to keep the Other's concerns out of the spotlight. He hates it that women turned issues of abortion, incest, and spousal abuse from private into public issues, that gays and lesbians successfully fought for legislation against "hate crimes," and that people of color demanded equal rights under the law and an end to institutional racism. Other legal and political attempts have been made—and are still being made—to secure the formal rights and liberties of previously disenfranchised groups and render establishmentarian institutions fueled by powerful prejudices accountable to the disempowered. The bigot responds by advocating a legal doctrine intent on recreating the "gilded age" of the late nineteenth century when women could not vote, segregation was the rule of thumb, and working people were under attack.[28]

Capitalist democracy shapes the rules of the game. Substantively exploitative and formally egalitarian, it is the economic-political system under which the bigot must operate. The economic arrangement rests on one basic principle, namely, that the interests of capital must be served prior to serving all other interests.[29] That is because, structurally, capital provides investment and investment determines employment. No investment—no employment. To this extent, substantively, labor and all other classes are dependent on capital under any version of the economic system known as capitalism. At the same time, however, capitalist democracy has a democratic element. Securing policies favorable to capital requires coalitional support from other larger classes and interests or disunity among those who might offer resistance to any given policies.[30]

This gives the bigot a card to play—and he has played his hand well. He now tends to highlight the formal elements of the rule of law and the need for protection against the intrusiveness of the state. He is even willing to applaud various successful representatives of subaltern groups. Still, he ignores how class cuts across identity constructions and how stark social and economic differences are growing within what were previously considered homogeneous groups like African Americans, Latinos, women, and others. He knows that a majority within each of these groups is suffering while a minority prospers.

The bigot can live with that. A study published by the Pew Charitable Trusts in July 2011 indicates that the median wealth of white households is now twenty times that of African American and eighteen times that of Hispanic households.[31] People of color find themselves dealing with incarceration, discriminatory hiring and lending practices, segregated neighborhoods, blatantly biased education funding, and—perhaps most strikingly—a health crisis. African Americans are twice as likely to die of a stroke as whites; twice as likely to suffer from diabetes; more than twice as likely to die of prostate cancer; and the numbers are only a bit less when it comes to breast cancer among women. In New York City, 72 percent of black males do not get their high school diplomas.[32] Put this all together and it becomes clear that class divisions and racial divisions tend to overlap and that there remain "two Americas."[33]

Structural imbalances of power do not excuse personal irresponsibility, apathy, or antisocial behavior. Conservatives are correct in emphasizing the need for individual initiative and the qualities required for individuals to overcome exploitative conditions. To deny this (whether intentionally or not) is to withdraw freedom from the subaltern and treat him as an object. Ignoring structural trends, however, is disingenuous. It lets the bigot formally call for assimilation of the Other (when he must), yet substantively deny that possibility through the policies he endorses. A study released on October 29, 2011, by the Bertelsmann Foundation showed that the United States has plummeted into the bottom five among the thirty leading industrial nations in "Overall Social Justice Rating," "Overall Poverty Prevention Rating," "Overall Poverty Rate," "Child Poverty Rate," and "Income Inequality." Such developments have had a real impact on the everyday lives of individuals. The culture of poverty has moved out of the ghetto and spilled over into the broader community.[34]

Condemnation of the "adversary culture" associated with the new social movements of the 1960s underpins the modern bigot's attempts to turn back the clock. But the stereotypes now seem to have taken on more of a class character. The white working class is apparently also using drugs, losing interest in education, engaging in crime, becoming sexually promiscuous, avoiding low-paying jobs—and going on welfare. Even the purely racial bias of the criminal justice system is witnessing the impact of both class distinctions within the black community as well as the growth of crime and incarceration within the working-class white community.[35] No longer is it only the welfare queen or those in the "hood" who should pull themselves up by their bootstraps. Class is ("surprisingly") becoming an increasingly important indicator of future educational success and low-income Americans have lesser chances of upward mobility than in most other economically advanced nations.[36] The economically disadvantaged also lack what has been termed social and cultural "capital" and the everyday habits and beliefs necessary for success.[37] So far as the bigot is concerned, however, the explanation for cultural and educational decline is obvious: the working class has become ever less white and ever less male.[38] The contagion has spread, thus confirming the bigot's original fears and resentments while conflating prejudice directed against the person as defined by color, ethnicity, or gender with the traditional contempt directed against the mob or the "lower classes."

Class analysis has always been distasteful to the bigot. When he tried to manipulate the German labor movement during the late nineteenth century, Frederick Engels and his friends sneered that anti-Semitism is "the socialism of fools." Retreat into the past became the bigot's response to capitalist democracy's transformation of his religious belief, his inherited wisdom, his chauvinism, into just another set of interests and interpretations. The growth of secularism and individualism only intensifies his feelings of isolation as well as bewilderment since he takes for granted what capitalist society provides and his prejudices cannot explain. Insofar as the inherently unproductive black underclass has (irrevocably?) tainted the inherently productive white industrial working class, the situation seems hopeless to the bigot. Any structural discussion of economic inequality only draws "us" apart and generates the kind of class conflict that undermines the national community.

But the bigot remains undeterred. He attempts to make use of a new ideological opportunity by oscillating between class and race and even gender in making his arguments. The supposedly colorblind capitalist does the same thing, as in the case of Mitt Romney who argued during the 2012 presidential campaign that "47 percent" of Americans are essentially freeloaders supported by the welfare state. It was clear to which audience he was playing. Just as the bigot had supported cuts in the welfare state, and the deregulation of the market and big business, establishmentarian conservatives favoring big business now indulged the true believer, the elitist, and the chauvinist. Indeed, there is a singular logic to this alliance.

Equitable distribution of wealth has statistically been shown to foster tolerance, promote a more robust and diverse civil society, and enhance the real life chances of the disadvantaged.[39] But focusing on economic structures, public policies, and political institutions is somehow less captivating than the slur by a celebrity or the whispered joke off-mike by a politician. Symbolism often causes more of a ruckus than policies that influence the subaltern's life. New media associated with the Internet, Facebook, Twitter, and the blogosphere consequently need to recast the symbolic character of the struggle against bigotry. Richard Thompson Ford put the matter well when he wrote, "In order to respond to the radical injustices of the new millennium, the civil rights movement will have to do more than broaden its agenda. It will need to change it, putting less emphasis on conspicuous racial animus and more on opaque, systemic, and often inadvertent causes of inequality, spending less time and energy on cathartic public demonstrations and more on institutional design."[40]

There should be no misunderstanding. Old-fashioned racism still exists; it underpins the new forms of unacknowledged bigotry. Traditional fears and assumptions about the supposedly criminal intentions of black youths bolstered by lack of legislation directed against easy access to handguns, "stand your ground laws" to protect private property and gated communities have resulted in any number of tragic cases of which the death of Trayvon Martin, and the acquittal in 2013 of the "neighborhood watch" volunteer who killed him, is only the most sensational. President Barack Obama poignantly stated that Trayvon Martin "could have been me thirty-five years ago" as he recalled being followed while shopping in a department store, hearing the click of car doors locking as he passed by, and seeing women clutching their handbags when he stepped into an elevator.

Resisting class exploitation is impossible without remembering the power of traditional bigotry and recognizing the need for solidarity among a wide range of subaltern groups. Parochial forms of identity politics and insular preoccupations with subjectivity are self-defeating. They threaten to turn each into the Other at any given time, over any given issue, as they compete for a shrinking economic pie. Intra-class tensions thereby result that only exacerbate (and are exacerbated by) traditional prejudices. The bigot delights in this kind of disunity: it compromises the struggle against him. But he senses the danger. Links between anti-racist and labor struggles have deep historical roots. The Civil Rights Movement aligned with union activism and the burgeoning Poor Peoples' Campaign.[41] With its famous march on Washington in 1969, hovering between a political party and an interest group, the Poor Peoples' Campaign remains perhaps the most vibrant expression of working-class protest against the imbalances of socioeconomic power since the New Deal. Coalitions have also recently emerged that associate the battle for gay rights with pro-immigrant and pro-labor legislation. In the presidential election of 2012, moreover, the Democratic Party received support from the great majority of citizens earning less than $50,000 along with 55 percent of women, 60 percent of voters between the ages of eighteen and twenty-nine, 73 percent of Asians, 71 percent of Latinos, and 93 percent of African Americans.[42] Worth noting is that 80 percent of Americans make under $84,000 a year and 60 percent make less than $52,000.

Many still believe that concern with issues of bigotry somehow deflects attention from the "real" issues of class conflict. The bigot knows better. He knows that the working class is increasingly no longer white and male and that, though exploitation is colorblind in principle, it tends to hit some elements or groups within the working class harder than others. Everyone knows that people of color would disproportionately suffer from a flat tax as well as other regressive attempts to shrink the tax base and, subsequently, bankrupt the welfare state. The same holds for questions of voting and political participation. It no longer makes sense to argue that group identity is antithetical to class interest or that cultural recognition of the Other has replaced economic redistribution of wealth as the remedy for injustice.[43] Concerns with the legal and cultural recognition of subaltern groups are becoming increasingly intertwined not merely with human rights but also with demands for social rights and economic justice. Gay couples want to get married and they want respect—but they also want a job. Social movements structured around identity rather than unions are now probably the primary sites from which class issues can be generated.

Categories like what I have termed the "class ideal" are required to coordinate and crystallize the general interests of working people in each social movement and identity group without arbitrarily privileging the concerns of any one in particular.[44] Of course, such concepts can easily be left hanging in the abstract. They require a referent in practice. The class ideal thus calls for frequent translation and retranslation into organizational and legislative demands and policies that will benefit the overriding class interests of subaltern groups. But intra-class solidarity and commitment to the class ideal cannot be imposed on social movements and identity groups from the outside in some modern version of vanguard thinking. Recognition of the Other and creation of a broader unity requires action by those working within existing interest groups and organizations mobilized around identity issues. Creating solidarity is the purpose of the class ideal. Any new approach will need to navigate and integrate three previously distinct facets of the struggle to marginalize the bigot: cultural practices that foster a cosmopolitan sensibility; political action that provides recognition for the disenfranchised and the outsider; and economic programs that privilege the class interests of working people.

Abolishing prejudice should inform all struggles against class exploitation. Changing demographics, greater diversity, global interdependence, secularism, new waves of immigration, and the growing power of the democratic idea offer new hopes for those seeking to challenge intolerance and defend the subaltern. At the same time, however, fighting the bigot is a labor of Sisyphus. Prejudice serves too many existential and material interests. It provides too many excuses for the loser, too many explanations for the ignorant, too much heroism for the coward, too much certainty for the disoriented, and too many justifications for the unearned privileges of times past.

No political or economic reform is secure and no cultural advance is safe from the bigot, who is always fighting on many fronts at once: the anthropological, the psychological, the social, and the political. These are incommensurate. Remedies that deal with one realm don't necessarily carry over when engaging another. The bigot is elusive. He appears in one arena only to disappear and then reappear elsewhere. Hatred is appealing and intolerance always remains in reserve. Old wounds continue to fester, old memories haunt the present, and old rumors will carry into the future. The bigot remains steadfast in resisting the prospects for a world in which all individuals insist on respect, equality, and social justice, knowing more, learning more, enjoying diversity—and living life as they choose. He knows his enemy. It is the same enemy the bigot has always had, namely, the idea that things can be different.

Appendix: Beginnings

During my many years at Rutgers University, I have taught any number of courses dealing with the politics of bigotry. They explored the prejudices experienced by different groups, the assumptions that unify them, and many of the themes dealt with in this volume. Students in groups are required to make in-class presentations: no one is allowed to present on the particular identity group to which he or she belongs. Each time I taught the course, it struck me how even many of my favorite students had never been exposed to the great names and classic works of the struggle against bigotry. More than one said to me: I never knew where to begin. So I thought it might be useful to close this book not with a bibliography in the usual sense but rather with some suggestions of well- and not-so-well-remembered literary works for further reading (and a few films). Not every form of intolerance is covered, and perhaps some of my choices are either too fashionable or hopelessly old-fashioned. Many of them can be considered under various rubrics and the list undoubtedly reveals my own biases. Still these mostly short, excellent works (complemented by selections from longer ones) might help teachers construct a syllabus that speaks to both the character of prejudice and the struggle against it. They will surely spark discussion among activist intellectuals and, if nothing else, offer the interested party a place to start.

Modernity

Literature: Immanuel Kant, "What Is Enlightenment?" (1784); Thomas Paine, "The Rights of Man" (1791); Karl Marx and Frederick Engels, *Communist Manifesto* (1848); Chinua Achebe, *Things Fall Apart* (1958).

Film: *The Man with a Movie Camera* (1929) directed by Dziga Vertov; *Wall Street* (1987) directed by Oliver Stone.

Anti-Semitism

Literature: William Shakespeare, *The Merchant of Venice* (1596–1598); Primo Levi, *Survival in Auschwitz* (1947); Jean-Paul Sartre, *Anti-Semite and Jew* (1946).

Film: *Gentleman's Agreement* (1947) directed by Elia Kazan; *Wannsee Conference* (1984) directed by Heinz Schirk.

Sexism

Literature: Mary Wollstonecraft, *Vindication of the Rights of Women* (1792); Simone de Beauvoir, *The Second Sex* (1949); Toni Morrison, *The Bluest Eye* (1970); Beverly LaHaye, *The Desires of a Woman's Heart* (1993).

Film: *A Brief Vacation* (1973) directed by Vittorio de Sica; *Swept Away* (1974) directed by Lina Wertmüller.

Racism

Literature: Ralph Ellison, *Invisible Man* (1952); James Baldwin, *The Fire Next Time* (1963); Lorraine Hansberry, *A Raisin in the Sun* (1959).

Film: *Birth of a Nation* (1915) directed by D. W. Griffith; *In the Heat of the Night* (1965) directed by Norman Jewison; *Do the Right Thing* (1989) directed by Spike Lee.

Gay Life

Literature: Thomas Mann, "Death in Venice" (1912); Jean Genet, *Our Lady of the Flowers* (1943); James Baldwin, *Giovanni's Room* (1956); Betty Berzon, *Surviving Madness* (2002).

Film: *Milk* (1977) directed by Gus Van Sant; *Kiss Me* (2012) directed by Alexandra-Therese Keining.

The True Believer

Literature: Fyodor Dostoyevsky, "The Grand Inquisitor" from *The Brothers Karamazov* (1882); Eric Hofer, *The True Believer* (1951); Arthur Miller, *The Crucible* (1953).

Film: *Inherit the Wind* (1960) directed by Stanley Kramer; *Gandhi* (1982) directed by Richard Attenborough.

The Elitist

Literature: Michael Oakeshott, "On Being Conservative" (1956); Leo Strauss, "What Is Liberal Education?" (1959); Ayn Rand, *The Virtue of Selfishness* (1964).

Film: *Joe* (1970) directed by John G. Avildsen; *The Ugly American* (1963) directed by George Englund.

The Chauvinist

Literature: Thomas Jefferson, "The Declaration of Independence" (1776); Sinclair Lewis, *Babbit* (1922); Samir Amin, *Eurocentrism* (2007); Samuel A. Huntington, "The Hispanic Challenge," *Foreign Policy* (2013).

Film: *Bad Day at Black Rock* (1955) directed by John Sturges; *West Side Story* (1961) directed by Robert Wise and Jerome Robbins.

Islamophobia

Literature: Edward Said, *Orientalism* (1979); Mahmood Mamdani, *Good Muslim, Bad Muslim* (2005); Samuel Huntington, "The Clash of Civilizations," *Foreign Affairs* (1993).

Film: *Exodus* (1960) directed by Otto Preminger; *Paradise Now* (2005) directed by Hany Abu-Assad.

Fanaticism

Literature: Albert Camus, "Caligula" (1939); George Mosse, ed., *Nazi Culture* (2003); William Luther Pierce, *The Turner Diaries* (1978).

Film: *Triumph of the Will* (1935) directed by Leni Riefenstahl; *Battle of Algiers* (1966) directed by Michel Pontecorvo.

Intolerance

Literature: John Locke, *A Letter Concerning Toleration* (1689);
   Voltaire, *Candide* (1759); Herbert Marcuse, *Repressive Tolerance* (1965).

Film: *To Kill a Mockingbird* (1962) directed by Robert Mulligan;
   Eyes on the Prize: America's Civil Rights Years, 1954–1964 (TV
   series) created by Henry Hampton.

Notes

Introduction

1. Gordon Allport, *The Nature of Prejudice* (Reading, MA: Addison Wesley, 1954), 9.
2. Cf. Elisabeth Young-Breuhl, *The Anatomy of Prejudices* (Cambridge, MA: Harvard University Press, 1998).
3. Wilhelm Reich, *The Mass Psychology of Fascism*, ed. Mary Higgens and Chester M. Raphael (New York: Farrar, Straus and Giroux, 1970), 47.
4. Note the discussion in Frederick Pollock, et al., *Group Experiment and Other Writings: The Frankfurt School on Public Opinion in Postwar Germany*, ed. and trans. Andrew J. Perrin and Jeffrey K. Olick (Cambridge, MA: Harvard University Press, 2012), 53.
5. T. W. Adorno et al., *The Authoritarian Personality* (New York: Harper, 1950), 605ff.
6. "Intercommunication between cultures in time and space is only possible because what makes men human is common

to them, and acts as a bridge between them. Our values are ours and theirs are theirs. We are free to criticize the values of other cultures, to condemn them, but we cannot pretend not to understand them at all or to regard them simply as subjective, the products of creatures in different circumstances with different tastes from our own, which do not speak to us at all." Isaiah Berlin, "The Pursuit of the Ideal," in *The Crooked Timber of Humanity: Chapters in the History of Ideas*, ed. Henry Hardy (New York: Vintage, 1992), 11.

7. The bigot's independence separates him from other partisans whose form of political organization serves as the crux of their identity and enables them to mobilize an "absolute" form of enmity against a particular opponent. Note the discussion by Carl Schmitt, *The Theory of the Partisan: Intermediate Commentary on the Concept of the Political*, trans. G. L. Ulmen (New York: Telos, 2007).

8. Samir Amin, *Eurocentrism*, 2d ed. (New York: Monthly Review Press, 2010), 166.

Chapter 1. Modernity

1. Karl Marx, *Capital: A Critique of Political Economy*, 3 vols., ed. Frederick Engels, trans. Samuel Moore and Edward Aveling (New York: International Publishers, 1967), 751.

2. Kenan Malik, "The Mirror of Race: Postmodernism and the Celebration of Difference," in Ellen Meiksins Wood and John Bellamy Foster, eds., *In Defense of History: Marxism and the Postmodern Agenda* (New York: Monthly Review Press, 1997), 127.

3. "After more than a century of claims that high intellectual or artistic accomplishment is somehow rooted in heredity and, more specifically, in the possession of 'genes for high

intelligence' or 'genes for creativity,' there is no credible evidence for their existence." Richard Lewontin, "Is There a Jewish Gene?" *New York Review of Books* (December 6, 2012), 18.

4. Discursive exclusion and relegating the Other "to silence does not simply correspond to (or is not simply reflective of) the relative powerlessness of black people at the time. It also reveals the evolving internal dynamics of the structure of modern discourse in the late seventeenth and eighteenth centuries in Western Europe—or during the Enlightenment." Cornel West, "Race and Modernity," in *The Cornel West Reader* (New York: Basic Civitas, 1999), 70.

5. Diana Judd, *Questioning Authority: Political Resistance and the Ethic of Natural Science* (New Brunswick, NJ: Transaction, 2009).

6. Marx to Arnold Ruge, September 1843, available at the Marxists Internet Archive, http://www.marxists.org/archive/marx/works/1843/letters/43_09-alt.htm (accessed September 29, 2013).

7. Karl Marx and Frederick Engels, *The Communist Manifesto*, ed. Jeffrey Isaac (with interpretive essays by Stephen Eric Bronner, Jeffrey Isaac, Saskia Sasson, and Vladimir Tismăneanu) (New Haven: Yale University Press, 2012), 76–77.

8. Karl Marx, "The Bourgeoisie and the Counter-Revolution," in Karl Marx and Frederick Engels, *Selected Works*, 3 vols. (New York: International Publishers, 1969), 1:138–142; Marx, "The Class Struggles in France, 1848–1850," in *Selected Works*, 1:186–300; Engels, Revolution and Counter-Revolution in Germany, in *Selected Works*, 1:300–388; and Marx, "The Eighteenth Brumaire of Louis Bonaparte," in *Selected Works*, 1:394–487.

9. Ibid., 1:406.

10. See Erich Fromm's analysis conducted during the late 1920s and early 1930s (when, it should be noted, social democracy was on the defensive and communism was entering its totalitarian phase): Fromm, *The Working Class in Germany: A Psychological and Sociological Study*, ed. Wolfgang Bonss (1939; Cambridge, MA: Harvard University Press, 1984).

11. This is true not only in the West. Note the discussion in Meera Nanda, *Prophets Facing Backward: Postmodern Critiques of Science and Hindu Nationalism in India* (New Brunswick, NJ: Rutgers University Press, 2003), 247ff.

12. Reich, *Mass Psychology of Fascism*, 15.

13. Inspired by "slave morality," resentment directs itself against what is different, creative, and unique, leading to a conformist definition of what is good, true, and beautiful. It thereby projects the failings of the inferior on an artificially constructed enemy. While Nietzsche viewed resentment as fundamental to all religious, democratic, and egalitarian movements, today it is expressed most by their opponents. Note the discussion by Friedrich Nietzsche in sections 10–11 of his *The Genealogy of Morals*, trans. Horace B. Samuel (New York: Dover, 2003), and Max Scheler, *Ressentiment* (Milwaukee, WI: Marquette University Press, 1994).

14. David Shapiro, *Neurotic Styles* (New York: Basic, 1999).

15. Theodor W. Adorno, *Guilt and Defense: On the Legacies of National Socialism in Germany*, ed. and trans. Jeffrey K. Olick and Andrew J. Perrin (Cambridge, MA: Harvard University Press, 2010), 115.

16. The wife of Tim LaHaye—the bombastic evangelical minister warning of apocalypse—makes her own hysterical pitch for stability and traditional marriage by noting that the hus-

band's authority is "not earned, not achieved, not dependent on superior intelligence, virtue or physical prowess, but assigned by God." Beverly LaHaye, *The Desires of a Woman's Heart: Encouragement for Women When Traditional Values Are Challenged* (Wheaten, IL: Tyndale House, 1993), 134.

17. Immanuel Kant, "Eternal Peace," in *Moral and Political Writings*, ed. Carl J. Friedrich (New York: Modern Library, 1949), 446.

18. See, in particular, the "World Values Survey" (1997) directed by Ronald Ingelhardt and the "Human Development Trends" analyzed by Hans Rostling, available at www.world valuessurvey.org; www.gapminder.org/downloads/human -development-trends-2005 (accessed October 25, 2013).

19. "The cosmopolitan sensibility presumes a certain capacity for empathy on the part of all individuals beyond the constraints imposed by their race, gender, or 'situation.' It assumes the existence of cultural differences and, from a critical standpoint, it celebrates the friction between the particular and the universal." Stephen Eric Bronner, *Ideas in Action: Political Tradition in the Twentieth Century* (Lanham, MD: Rowman & Littlefield, 1999), 333.

20. From the fine novel *The Prague Cemetery* by Umberto Eco, trans. Richard Dixon (New York: Houghton Mifflin, 2011), 6.

21. See Martin Heidegger, *Being and Time*, trans. John Macquarrie and Edward Robinson (New York: Harper & Row, 1962), 167–169.

22. Eco, *Prague Cemetery*, 17.

23. Legitimizing the status of the bigot requires devaluing the subaltern. "These two attempts at legitimacy are actually inseparable. Moreover, the more the usurped is downtrodden, the more the usurper triumphs and, thereafter, con-

firms his guilt and establishes his self-condemnation. Thus the momentum of this mechanism for defense propels itself and worsens as it continues to move. This self-defeating process pushes the usurper to go one step further; to wish the disappearance of the usurped, whose very existence causes him to take the role of usurper, and whose heavier and heavier oppression makes him more and more of an oppressor himself." Albert Memmi, *The Colonizer and the Colonized*, trans. Howard Greenfield (Boston: Beacon Press, 1991), 51.

24. Henri Parens, "The Roots of Prejudice: Findings from Observational Research," in Parens, *The Future of Prejudice: Psychoanalysis and the Prevention of Prejudice* (Lanham, MD: Rowman & Littlefield, 2007), 23.

25. Herbert Marcuse, "Repressive Tolerance," in *A Critique of Pure Tolerance* (Boston: Beacon, 1969).

26. Stephen Eric Bronner, "Critical Intellectuals, Politics, and Society," in *Imagining the Possible: Radical Politics for Conservative Times* (New York: Routledge, 2002), 73ff.

27. Cited in Sir Isaiah Berlin, "Joseph de Maistre and the Origins of Fascism," in *The Crooked Timber of Humanity* (New York: Vintage, 1992), 100.

28. Zev Sternhell, *The Anti-Enlightenment Tradition*, trans. David Maisel (New Haven: Yale University Press, 2009), 216.

29. Cf. Nadia Abu El-Haj, *The Genealogical Science: The Search for Jewish Origins and the Politics of Epistemology* (Chicago: University of Chicago Press, 2012).

30. See the intellectual biography Nahum N. Glatzer, *Franz Rosenzweig: His Life and Thought* (New York: Hackett, 1998).

31. Benedict Anderson, *Imagined Communities: Reflections on the Origin and Spread of Nationalism* (London: Verso, 2006).

32. Tzevetan Todorov, *The Fear of Barbarians*, trans. Andrew Brown (Chicago: University of Chicago Press, 2010), 34.

33. Melissa V. Harris-Perry, *Sister Citizen: Shame, Stereotypes, and Black Women in America* (New Haven: Yale University Press, 2011), 38.

34. Frances Fox Piven, *Challenging Authority: How Ordinary People Change America* (Lanham, MD: Rowman & Littlefield, 2006), 146.

Chapter 2. Mythological Thinking

1. "Amputations and Killings Shake an Embattled Mali," *New York Times* (September 11, 2012), A8.

2. Jürgen Habermas, *The Liberating Power of Symbols: Philosophical Essays*, trans. Peter Dews (Cambridge: MIT Press, 2001), 11–15.

3. Laurie A. Rudman, "Rejection of Women? Beyond Prejudice as Antipathy," in *On the Nature of Prejudice: Fifty Years after Allport* (Oxford: Blackwell, 2005), 106ff.

4. Lizzy Ratner, "The War between Civilized Man and Pamela Geller," *The Nation* (October 18, 2012).

5. Gordon Willard Allport, *The Nature of Prejudice* (New York: Perseus Books, 1979), 109.

6. Ibid., 196.

7. Theodor Adorno et al., *The Authoritarian Personality* (New York: Harper & Row, 1950), 353.

8. Paul Sims, "Demonizing Muslims," *The New Humanist* (July–August 2011): 15ff.

9. Quoted in Erich Fromm, *Escape from Freedom* (New York: Henry Holt, 1965), 228–229.

10. *New York Times* (July 5, 2007).

11. David Hallett Fischer, *Historians' Fallacies: Toward a Logic of Historical Thought* (New York: Harper, 1970), 74–78.

12. Frances Fox Piven, *Who's Afraid of Frances Fox Piven?* (New York: New Press, 2011), 237ff.

13. Karl Marx, "The Fetishism of Commodities and the Secret Thereof," in *Capital: The Critique of Political Economy*, 3 vols., ed. Frederick Engels, trans. Samuel Moore and Edward Aveling (New York: International Publishers, 1967), 1:71ff.

14. Richard Hofstadter, *The Paranoid Style in American Politics* (New York: Vintage, 1967), 37–38.

15. Kathryn S. Olmstead, *Real Enemies: Conspiracy Theories and American Democracy, World War I to 9/11* (New York: Oxford University Press, 2009), 8ff.

16. "Pakistani Girl, a Global Heroine after an Attack, Has Critics at Home," *New York Times* (October 12, 2013), A4.

17. All quotations are from the chapter "Anti-Semitism for Popular Consumption: Selections from the Protocols of the Elders of Zion," in ibid., 11–31.

18. The same holds for the notorious "blood libel," whose scene shifts—as circumstances dictate—from Europe to Russia to the Middle East.

19. Hannah Arendt, *The Origins of Totalitarianism* (Cleveland: Meridian, 1958), 7.

20. David Norman Smith, "The Social Construction of Enemies: Jews and the Representation of Evil," *Sociological Theory* 14, no. 3 (November 1996): 222.

21. Ernst Cassirer, *Language and Myth* (New York: Dover, 1953), 58.

22. Chrystia Freeland, "Super Rich Irony: Why Do America's Billionaires Feel Victimized by Obama?" *New Yorker* (October 8, 2012).

23. The citation, which was written following the prisoner exchange of Gilad Shalit for 1,027 Palestinian prisoners toward the end of 2011, appears in Eric Alterman, "Attack Dog Jennifer Rubin Muddies the Washington Post's Reputation," *The Nation* (June 27, 2012).

24. It is worth noting that *Exodus* was expressly commissioned by a New York public relations firm to bolster Israel's image in the United States. See the Introduction to Matthew Abraham, *Out of Bounds: Academic Freedom and the Question of Palestine* (New York: Bloomsbury Academic, 2014).

25. Edward Said, "Permission to Narrate," *London Review of Books* 6, no. 3 (February 16, 1984): 13–17.

26. Robert Fisk, "Priouettes of an Ex-Visionary," *The Independent* (July 9, 1994).

27. Henri Parens, "Toward Understanding Prejudice—Benign and Malignant," in Henri Parens, Afaf Mahfouz, Stuart W. Twemlow, and David E. Scharff, eds., *The Future of Prejudice: Psychoanalysis and the Prevention of Prejudice* (Lanham, MD: Rowman & Littlefield, 2007), 21–36.

28. "Power is indeed of the essence of all government, but violence is not. Violence is by nature instrumental; like all means, it always stands in need of guidance and justification through the end it pursues. And what needs justification by something else cannot be the essence of anything." Hannah Arendt, *On Violence* (New York: Harcourt, 1970), 51.

29. The FBI, once considered an ally, was by 1971 considered by the KKK and white power leaders like Andrew Macdonald to be part of the corrupt and degenerate system. See John Drabble, "From White Supremacy to White Power: The FBI, COINTELPRO-White Hate and the Nazification of the Ku Klux Klan in the 1970s," *American Studies* 48,

no. 3 (Fall 2007): 49–74. The *Turner Diaries*, published in 1978, was named "the bible of the racist right" in Southern Poverty Law Center, Intelligence Report (Fall 2004).

30. Rob McAlear, "Hate, Narrative, and Propaganda in *The Turner Diaries*," in *Journal of American Culture* 32, no. 3 (2009): 192, 200.

31. The idea that liberal politics has been generated by fanaticism is fashionable but deeply mistaken. Enlightenment political thought is actually less a response to religion than is the religious fanaticism that Europe inherited from the Peasant Wars. The need to distinguish between arbitrary and legitimate authority, so crucial to liberal thought, is irrelevant to the fanatic. To be sure, enough liberals and socialists strayed from principle but, in principle, liberal democracy rests on constraining arbitrary power, while the fanatic is willing to attain his aims by any means necessary. Cf. Alberto Toscano, *Fanaticism: On the Uses of an Idea* (London: Verso, 2010).

32. "Many of Breivik's ideas are common amongst the electorate in Norway and in the rest of Europe and mainstream political parties are to blame for not confronting racism, sexism, and ignorance in debates about immigration and integration." Mette Wigen, "Rethinking Anti-Immigration Rhetoric after the Oslo and Utoya Terrorist Attacks," *New Political Science* 34, no. 4 (December 2012): 585–587.

33. Andrew Macdonald, *The Turner Diaries* (Fort Lee, NJ: Barricade Books, 1996), 71.

34. Smith, "Social Construction of Enemies," 217.

35. Pamela Geller's comment is from *New York Times* (July 25, 2011).

36. Brad Whitsel, "The Turner Diaries and Cosmotheism: Wil-

liam Turner's Theology," in *Journal of Alternative and Emergent Religions* 1, no. 2 (April 1998): 188ff.

37. Incendiary works abound: cf. Bruce Bawer, *While Europe Slept: How Radical Islam Is Destroying the West from Within* (New York: Anchor, 2007); Melanie Phillips, *Londonistan* (London: Encounter, 2007); and Robert Spencer, *The Truth about Muhammad: Founder of the World's Most Intolerant Religion* (Washington, DC: Regnery, 2006).

Chapter 3. Playing the Role

1. Herbert Marcuse, "The Affirmative Character of Culture" (1937), in Marcuse, *Negations: Essays in Critical Theory*, trans. Jeremy J. Shapiro (Boston: Beacon, 1969), 95.

2. Jürgen Habermas, *The Liberating Power of Symbols: Philosophical Essays*, trans. Peter Dews (Cambridge, MA: MIT Press, 2001), 13ff.

3. Provincialism can also be understood in a positive light. Attempts to secure the customs of a particular province are juxtaposed against a more virulent xenophobic parochialism by Josiah Royce, *Race Questions, Chauvinism, and Other American Problems* (New York: MacMillan, 1908).

4. Theodor W. Adorno, *Critical Models: Interventions and Catchwords*, trans. Henry W. Pickford (New York: Columbia University Press, 1998), 167–168.

5. "The superego of an epoch of civilization has an origin similar to that of an individual . . . I would not say that an attempt to carry psychoanalysis over to the cultural community was absurd or doomed to be fruitless. But we should have to be very cautious and not forget that, after all, we are only dealing with analogies and that it is dangerous, not only with men but also with concepts, to tear them from the

sphere in which they originated and been evolved." Sigmund Freud, *Civilization and Its Discontents*, trans. James Strachey (New York, W. W. Norton, 1961), 88, 91.

6. Wilhelm Reich, *The Mass Psychology of Fascism*, ed. Mary Higgins and Chester M. Raphael (New York: Farrar, Straus and Giroux, 1970), 30.

7. Joseph Sandler with Anna Freud, *The Analysis of Defense: The Ego and the Mechanisms of Defense Revisited* (New York: International Universities Press, 1985), 432.

8. Erich Fromm, *Escape from Freedom* (London: Farrar and Rinehart, 1941), 276.

9. Ibid., 169.

10. Jean-Paul Sartre, *Being and Nothingness*, trans. Hazel Barnes (New York: Philosophical Library, 1965), 65.

11. Freud, *Civilization and Its Discontents*, 23.

12. Wilhelm Reich, *The Mass Psychology of Fascism* (London: Farrar, Straus and Giroux, 1933), 15.

13. Fromm, *Escape from Freedom*, 121.

14. Ibid., 136.

15. Reich, *The Mass Psychology of Fascism*, 37.

16. T. W. Adorno, *Prisms*, trans. Samuel and Shierry Weber (Cambridge, MA: MIT Press, 1983).

17. Freud, *Civilization and Its Discontents*, 56.

18. Leo Lowenthal and Norbert Guterman, "Prophets of Deceit," in Lowenthal, *False Prophets: Studies on Authoritarianism* (New Brunswick, NJ: Transaction, 1987), 27.

19. On Huckabee, see *The Huffington Post* (October 12, 2012); on Pat Robertson, see Robertson's CNN newscast on January 13, 2010; on the views of many Orthodox rabbis, see The American Council for Judaism, *Special Interest Report* (May–June 2007).

20. Martha Nussbaum, *The New Religious Intolerance: Overcoming the Politics of Fear in an Anxious Age* (Cambridge, MA: Harvard University Press, 2012).

21. P. B. Wilson, *Liberated through Submission: God's Design for Freedom in All Relationships* (Eugene, OR: Harvest House, 1990).

22. Each nation has its own charlatans and frauds but no one has depicted the shyster evangelist with more cynical clarity and socio-psychological acumen than Sinclair Lewis in his sensational novel *Elmer Gantry* (1927).

23. See the illuminating analysis in Cullen Murphy, *God's Jury: The Inquisition and the Making of the Modern World* (New York: Houghton Mifflin, 2012).

24. See John Toland, *Adolf Hitler* (New York: Doubleday, 1976), 222.

25. Johann Wolfgang von Goethe, *Dichtung und Wahrheit*, in *Werke*, vol. 5 (Frankfurt: Insel, 1981), 5:125.

26. Philip Kitcher, *Abusing Science: The Case against Creationism* (Cambridge, MA: MIT Press, 1983), and Kitcher, *Living with Darwin: Evolution, Design, and the Future of Faith* (New York: Oxford University Press, 2007).

27. Karl Marx, "Toward the Critique of Hegel's Philosophy of Law: Introduction" in *Writings of the Young Marx on Philosophy and Society*, ed. and trans. Loyd D. Easton and Kurt H. Guddat (New York: Doubleday, 1967), 250. Emphasis in the original.

28. Charles Murray, *Real Education: Four Simple Truths for Bringing America's Schools Back to Reality* (New York: Three Rivers, 2009).

29. Edmund Burke, *Reflections on the Revolution in France*, ed. Frank M. Turner (New Haven: Yale University Press, 2003), 66.

30. Corey Robin, *The Reactionary Mind: Conservatism from Edmund Burke to Sarah Palin* (Oxford: Oxford University Press, 2011), 8.

31. Cornel West, "Nihilism in Black America," in West, *Race Matters* (Boston: Beacon Press, 2001).

32. This policy was initially the response embraced by moderate Republicans to the radicalism of the new social movements and their demand for what might be termed "class action." See Alba Alexander, Stephen Eric Bronner, and Kurt Jacobsen, "Affirmative Action Politics," *Critical Sociology* 23, no. 13 (1998): 85–102.

33. Dinesh D'Souza, *The End of Racism* (New York: Free Press, 1995), 489.

34. Samir Amin, *Eurocentrism* (New York: Monthly Review Press, 2009), 180.

35. Friedrich Pollock, *Group Experiment* (Cambridge, MA: Harvard University Press, 2011), 115.

36. Michael Oakeshott, "On Being Conservative," in Oakeshott, *Rationalism in Politics and Other Essays* (New York: Harper, 1962).

37. Albert O. Hirschman, *The Rhetoric of Reaction: Perversity, Futility, Jeopardy* (Cambridge, MA: Harvard University Press, 1991).

38. Note the fine study by R. Claire Snyder, *Gay Marriage and Democracy: Equality for All* (Lanham, MD: Rowman & Littlefield, 2006).

39. W. E. B. Du Bois, *Dusk at Dawn: An Essay toward an Autobiography of a Race Concept* (New Brunswick, NJ: Transaction, 1997), 99.

40. Salmon Akhtar, "From Unmentalized Xenophobia to Messianic Sadism: Some Reflections on the Phenomenology,"

in Parens, Mahfouz, Twemlow, and Scharff, *Future of Prejudice*, 9.

41. Lowenthal and Guterman, "Prophets of Deceit," 78.

42. Note the excellent study by Russell Jacoby: *Bloodlust: On the Roots of Violence from Cain and Abel to the Present* (New York: Free Press, 2011).

43. Propaganda by both sides in World War I pitted the supposed romantic depth of German *Kultur* against the supposed rationalist frippery of French "civilization." This juxtaposition is reflected in the famous controversy between Thomas Mann, who wrote *Confessions of a Non-Political Man*, and his brother Heinrich Mann, who responded with *Confessions of a Political Man*. Note the discussion in Stephen Eric Bronner, *Reclaiming the Enlightenment* (New York: Columbia University Press, 2004), 117–119.

44. "Enlightenment is man's leaving his self-caused immaturity. Immaturity is the incapacity to use one's intelligence without the guidance of another. Such immaturity is self-caused if it is not caused by lack of intelligence but by lack of determination and courage to use one's intelligence without being guided by another. *Sapere Aude!* 'Have the courage to use your own intelligence!' is therefore the motto of the enlightenment." Immanuel Kant, "What Is Enlightenment? In *Moral and Political Writings*, ed. Carl J. Friedrich (New York: Modern Library, 1949), 132.

45. Richard C. Sennett, *The Fall of Public Man* (New York: Knopf, 1977).

46. A new romantic and secular notion of German identity emerged in the nineteenth century that was directed not to the elites but the masses: it involved responding to the imperialist ambitions of Napoleon, while opposing citizenship

for Jews. See J. G. Fichte, *Addresses to the German Nation*, ed. Gregory Moore (Cambridge: Cambridge University Press, 2008).

47. Pollock, *Group Experiment*, 64–65.
48. Sigmund Freud, *Group Psychology and the Analysis of the Ego*, trans. James Strachey (New York: International Psycho-Analytical Press, 1923), 64.
49. Lowenthal and Guterman, "Prophets of Deceit," 60.
50. Ethan J. Kyle and Balin Roberts, "Still Fighting the Civil War in South Carolina," *L.A. Progressive* (December 18, 2010).
51. Leo Lowenthal, "Toward a Psychology of Authoritarianism," in Lowenthal, *False Prophets*, 262.
52. "You murder Negroes, so you cannot reproach us for having murdered Jews, if not even: You actually showed us how." Cited in Theodor W. Adorno, *Guilt and Defense: On the Legacies of National Socialism in Postwar Germany*, trans. Jeffrey K. Olick and Andrew J. Perrin (Cambridge, MA: Harvard University Press, 2012), 126.
53. Olivier Roy, *Secularism Confronts Islam*, trans. George Holoch (New York: Columbia University Press, 2007), 69.

Chapter 4. The Bigot Today

1. James Baldwin, "My Dungeon Shook," in Baldwin, *The Fire Next Time* (New York: Vintage, 1993), 6.
2. Walter Benjamin, "The Work of Art in the Age of Mechanical Reproduction," in Benjamin, *Illuminations*, ed. Hannah Arendt and trans. Harry Zohn (New York: Shocken, 1968), 217.
3. Michelle Alexander, *The New Jim Crow: Mass Incarceration in the Age of Color-Blindness* (New York: New Press, 2012).

4. For the Saudi Arabia beheading, see the CNN report at www.cnn.com/2011/12/13/world/meast/saudi-arabia -beheading (accessed October 27, 2013). For the attack by Israeli teens, see the article in *Haaretz* (August 20, 2012).

5. UN News Centre, "UN Issues First Report on Human Rights of Gay and Lesbian People," December 15, 2011, available at the UN News Centre website, http://www.un .org/apps/news/story.asp?NewsID=40743#.UkgOsT8 mydk (accessed September 29, 2013).

6. Ministère de l'Intérieur: "Résultats de l'élection présiden-tielle 2012," April 22 and May 6, 2012, available at the French Interior Ministry website, http://www.interieur.gouv.fr/ Elections/Les-resultats/Presidentielles/elecresult _PR2012/%28path%29/PR2012/index.html (accessed Sep-tember 29, 2013).

7. Damien McElroy: "Golden Dawn Takes Advantage of Re-cession Ravaged Greece," *The (London) Telegraph* (Novem-ber 2, 2012).

8. Norman Podhoretz, "The Adversary Culture and the New Class," in Podhoretz, *The Bloody Crossroads: Where Litera-ture and Politics Meet* (New York: Simon & Schuster, 1986), 115–135.

9. "For if it is true that no production of knowledge in the human sciences can ever ignore or disclaim its author's in-volvement as a human subject in his own circumstances, then it must also be true that for a European or American studying the Orient there can be no disclaiming the main circumstances of his actuality: that . . . [he] belongs to a power with definite interests in the Orient, and more im-portant, that one belongs to a part of the earth with a defi-nite history of involvement in the Orient almost since the

time of Homer." Edward Said, *Orientalism* (New York: Random House, 1979), 10.

10. Stephen Eric Bronner, "Constructing Neo-Conservatism," in *Blood in the Sand: Imperial Fantasies, Right-Wing Ambitions, and the Erosion of American Democracy* (Lexington: University of Kentucky Press, 2005), 119ff.

11. For more, see Arthur Schlesinger, Jr., *The Vital Center: The Politics of Freedom* (Boston: Houghton Mifflin, 1949).

12. Seymour Martin Lipset, *The Politics of Unreason: Right-Wing Extremism in America, 1790–1977* (Chicago: University of Chicago Press, 1977).

13. Theda Skocpol and Vanessa Williamson, *The Tea Party and the Remaking of Republican Conservatism* (New York: Oxford University Press, 2012).

14. There are fine articles on the subject: see, for example, Michael J. Thompson, "Suburban Origins of the Tea Party: Spatial Dimensions of the New Conservative Personality"; Lauren Langman, "Cycles of Contention: The Rise and Fall of the Tea Party"; and Chip Berlet, "Collectivists, Communists, Organized Labor Bosses, Bankers, and Subversion: How Organized Wealth Promotes Counter-Subversion Panics," all in *Critical Sociology* 38, no. 4 (July 2012).

15. Jill Lepore, *The Whites of Their Eyes: The Tea Party's Revolution and the Battle over American History* (Princeton, NJ: Princeton University Press, 2010).

16. *The Economist* (March 10, 2012), 40.

17. Sam Tanenhaus, "Will the Tea Get Cold?" *New York Review of Books* (March 8, 2012), 7ff.

18. Tom Grieve, "Ann Coulter: Someone Should Poison Justice Stevens," *Salon* (January 27, 2006); "Official Stirs Texas City with Talk of Rebellion," *New York Times* (August 29, 2012),

A15; "Sarah Palin Criticized for Presence of Gabrielle Giffords on 'Target List,'" available at CBSNews.com, http://www.cbsnews.com/8301-503544_162-20027918-503544.html (accessed October 27, 2013).

19. Geoffrey Kabaservice, *Rule and Ruin: The Downfall of Moderation and the Destruction of the Republican Party, from Eisenhower to the Tea Party* (New York: Oxford University Press, 2012).

20. On Romney, Rove, and Morris, respectively, see the *Huffington Post* online at www.huffingtonpost.com/2012/.../mitt-romney-obama-gifts_n_2133529.html; www.huffingtonpost.com/2012/...karl-rove-obama-suppressing-voten_n_2094459.html; www.huffingtonpost.com/2012/.../karl-rove-obama-suppressing. www.foxnews.com/on-air/.../2012/.../dick-morris-romney-will-win-landslide; on Coulter, see "Ann Coulter's Disastrous Political Strategy: 'Take Away Women's Right to Vote,'" ThinkProgress.org, October 4, 2007, http://thinkprogress.org/media/2007/10/04/16751/coulter-gardner (all accessed October 28, 2013).

21. Conor Fredersdorf, "Almost Half of Republicans Indulge the 'Stolen Election' Delusion," *The Atlantic* (December 6, 2012).

22. Note the study by Nicholas Carnes, *White-Collar Government: The Hidden Role of Class in Economic Policy Making* (Chicago: University of Chicago Press, 2013).

23. Richard C. Sennett, *Together: The Rituals, Pleasures, and Politics of Cooperation* (New Haven: Yale University Press, 2012).

24. Jean-Paul Sartre, *The Words*, trans. Bernard Frechtman (New York: George Braziller, 1964), 255.

25. Ian Buruma, "Living with Islam," *New York Review of Books* (May 14, 2009), 13.

26. With respect to the U.S. Supreme Court, indeed, it has been argued that racism is mostly perpetuated through decisions that make no conscious reference to race, whereas those decisions that highlight race usually attempt to mitigate discriminatory practices. Ian F. Haney Lopez, "Institutional Racism: Judicial Conduct and a New Theory of Racial Discrimination," *Yale Law Journal* 109, no. 8 (June 2000), 1717ff.

27. See the classic work originally published in 1960 by C. Wright Mills, *The Sociological Imagination* (New York: Oxford University Press, 2000).

28. David R. Dow, "Impeaching the Supreme Court Justices," *Daily Beast* (April 4, 2012).

29. Joshua Cohen and Joel Rogers, *On Democracy: Toward a Transformation of American Society* (New York: Penguin, 1983).

30. That is the political reality of a situation in which, according to the Center on Budget and Policy Priorities (September 9, 2009), available online at www.cbpp.org, two-thirds of the nation's total income gains from 2002 to 2007 flowed to the top 1 percent of U.S. households. The last time such a large share of the income gain went to the top 1 percent of households—and such a small share went to the bottom 90 percent of households—was in the 1920s.

31. Rakesh Kochhar et al., "Wealth Gaps Rise to Record Highs between Whites, Blacks, Hispanics," *Pew Foundation* (July 26, 2011), available at the Pew Foundation website, http://www.pewsocialtrends.org/2011/07/26/wealth-gaps-rise-to-record-highs-between-whites-blacks-hispanics (accessed September 29, 2013).

32. Helen Epstein, "Children of the Storm," *The Nation* (December 3, 2012), 33.

33. Tavis Smiley and Cornel West, *The Rich and the Rest of Us: A Poverty Manifesto* (New York: SmileyBooks, 2012).

34. Charles Murray, *Coming Apart: The State of White America, 1960–2010* (New York: Crown, 2012).

35. James Forman, Jr., "Racial Critiques of Mass Incarceration: Beyond the New Jim Crow" (2012) in Yale Faculty Scholarship Series, paper no. 3599, available online at http://digital commons.law.yale.edu/fss_papers/3599 (accessed October 27, 2013). Thanks to my colleague Lisa Miller for bringing this article to my attention.

36. *New York Times* (December 23, 2012), n.p.

37. Richard Sennett and Jonathan Cobb, *The Hidden Injuries of Class* (New York: W. W. Norton, 1993), 51–53.

38. Opposition to compensatory policies like affirmative action is associated not with the oft-proclaimed vision of a color-blind society but instead, as empirical studies consistently show, with support for hierarchical and nonegalitarian values. See James Sidanius et al., "It's Not Affirmative Action, It's the Blacks: The Continuing Relevance of Race in American Politics," in David O. Sears, James Sidanius, and Lawrence Bobo, eds., *Racialized Politics* (Chicago: University of Chicago Press, 1999), 191–235.

39. Note the manifold statistics offered in Richard Wilkinson and Kate Pickett, *The Spirit Level: Why Greater Equality Makes Societies Stronger* (London: Bloomsbury Press, 2009).

40. Richard Thompson Ford, "When We Talk about Race," *New York Times Book Review* (July 3, 2011), 12.

41. Note the seminal study by Frances Fox Piven and Richard

Cloward, *Poor Peoples' Movements: Why They Succeed, How They Fail* (New York: Vintage, 1978).

42. Roper Center of the University of Connecticut, "How Groups Voted in 2012," available at www.ropercenter.uconn .edu/elections/how_groups_voted/voted/12.html (accessed October 28, 2013).

43. Nancy Fraser, "From Redistribution to Recognition? Dilemmas of Justice in a Post-Socialist Age," *New Left Review* (July–August 1995): 68–93.

44. Stephen Eric Bronner, *Socialism Unbound: Principles, Practices, and Prospects*, 2d ed. (New York: Columbia University Press, 2011), 164ff.

Index

ACORN, 176
Action Française, 43–44
Adorno, Theodor W., 102, 110
affirmative action, 17, 128, 221n38
African Americans, 32, 47, 50, 60–61,
140, 149, 171–72, 186–87
Akhtar, Salmon, 138
Allport, Gordon, 148
America First, 166
American Conservative Union, 174
American Freedom Defense Initia-
tive, 61
Anderson, Benedict, 46
Anthony, Susan B., 48
Antichrist, 33
anti-Semitism, 33, 37–38, 44, 58, 66,
74–85, 144, 189
anxiety, 104, 106, 110–11, 161
apocalypse, 67, 90, 95, 97

Arabs, 62, 79, 84, 144, 163. *See also*
Muslims
Arendt, Hannah, 78–79, 81, 209n28
aristocracy, 19, 128–29, 144
armed forces, gays in, 62
Armey, Dick, 167
Aryan Nation, 26
Atlas Shrugs (web site), 96
Augustine, Saint, 126
authenticity, 35, 37–38, 45
authoritarianism, 8, 64, 94, 102–3,
125, 130
authority, 16, 37, 103, 110, 204n16

Babeuf, François Noël, 72
Bachmann, Michele, 171
bad faith, 38, 109
Bakker, Jim and Tammy Faye, 116
Baldwin, James, 154, 181

Barrès, Maurice, 42–44, 136, 141, 143
Beaumarchais, Pierre, 23
Beauvoir, Simone de, 39–40
Beck, Glenn, 2, 69
belonging, 103, 141–42, 148–49, 153
Benjamin, Walter, 155
Berlin, Isaiah, 201n6
Bible. *See* Scripture
bigots and bigotry: adaptability and
    elusiveness of, 11–12, 32, 55, 178,
    194–95; adversaries of, 8–9, 21–22,
    26–37, 57–58, 63, 74; camouflaging
    of, 154–64; characteristics of, 4–5,
    8, 86; combating, 3–4, 12, 104,
    151, 161, 178–95; conservatism
    of, 155–57, 164; contemporary,
    154–95; ego of, 8, 28, 107, 202n7
    goal of, 8; interests and principles
    of, 11, 17, 58, 165, 168, 171;
    internalization of, 46; personal, vs.
    political, perspective on, 179–80;
    phenomenology of, 4; psychology
    of, 5–7, 22–23, 110; roles of, 5–6, 8,
    99–153; settings for, 8, 21, 106–7;
    targets of, 4, 5, 26, 156–57; threats
    to, 5, 9, 25, 27; victimhood of, 23,
    70, 95, 97; world of, 5–7, 9, 22, 24,
    46, 63, 100–101, 105, 106, 148–49
Bilderberg banking group, 69
binary oppositions, 24, 105, 112, 119,
    156, 181–82
Black Power, 50
blood (ancestry), 44–45, 142
Bonaparte, Napoleon, 130, 215n46
Bork, Robert, 184

Bourget, Paul, 43
Brecht, Bertolt, 30
Breivik, Anders Behring, 90–93, 96
Brown v. Board of Education, 184
Brundtland, Gro Harlem, 91
Buddhism, 25
Burke, Edmund, 127, 128
Buruma, Ian, 183
Bush, George W., 162–63

Caesar, Irving, 149
Cain, Herman, 171
Camus, Albert, 38, 46, 123
capitalism: challenge represented by,
    17–20, 189; community eroded by,
    148; and democracy, 185–86; fear
    of, 17; fundamentalism about, 170;
    and liberalism, 18; margins of, 21;
    and modernity, 14, 17–20; nostalgic
    view of, 144, 146; principles of, 185
Cassirer, Ernst, 81
Catiline, 71
Caves of the Patriarchs massacre
    (1994), 96
Central Intelligence Agency (CIA),
    70
Chamberlain, Houston S., 136–37
change: absent from mythological
    thinking, 54–56; anxiety about,
    106–7; bigots' encounter with,
    155–56; confusion caused by,
    29–30, 113–14, 145–46; elitists'
    opposition to, 132, 134–36;
    resistance to, 9, 21, 37, 183–84,
    195; as threat, 94–95

Index

charisma, 97, 117, 130

chauvinists, 5–6, 141–53; bewilderment of, 145, 189; bigoted forms of, 102–3; challenges to, 151–53; and community, 141–53; cosmopolitanism vs., 141–42, 156, 165; economic viewpoint of, 146–47; enemies of, 111–12; and the family, 143; and liberalism, 147; nostalgia of, 144–46, 151; positive aspects of, 101; sense of belonging important to, 141–42; in the South, 149–50; strangers as threat to, 148–49; in Tea Party, 168; thoughts and opinions of, 100, 110–11; and tradition, 142, 153; and women, 143

Chesterfield, Lord, 59

Chinese, 61, 69

Christianity, 25, 30, 33, 118, 129

circular reasoning, 62–63, 78, 130, 135

civility, 180–81

civilization, 25, 31, 52, 62, 87, 91. See also society

civil rights, 48, 124, 180

Civil Rights Act (1964), 162, 184

Civil Rights Movement, 47, 161, 183, 190, 192

Civil War, 149–50

class, 19, 188–89, 191–94

Clementi, Tyler, 2

climate change, 164

Cloward, Richard, 69

colonialism, 28, 40, 60, 140. See also imperialism

color-blind attitudes and policies, 155, 169, 180, 189, 220n26, 221n38

community: authoritarian, 103; capitalist erosion of, 148; chauvinism and, 100, 141–53; foundational role of, 21; identity politics and, 48; identity rooted in, 44–46; imagined, 46; mythological thinking and, 55; nostalgia for, 106; protection of, 18, 22, 24, 33, 43, 46; reactionary conception of, 17–18, 42, 44; small-town, 147–48

compensatory policies, 128, 132, 140–41, 221n38

Confederacy, 149–50, 173

conformity, 7, 95, 97, 103, 131

Confucius, 25

confusion, 29–30, 113–14, 145–46

conscience, 6, 60, 87–89

conservatism, 127, 132, 137, 155–57, 159, 164, 187. See also establishmentarian conservatism; neoconservatism

conspiracy fetishism, 68–86, 164

Constitution, U.S., 183–85

cosmopolitanism: absence of, 146; as antidote to bigotry, 104, 181; chauvinism vs., 141–42, 156, 165; constraints imposed by, 183; defined, 205n19; liberalism and, 182; modernity and, 25, 44, 106, 168; and the Other, 181–82; and personal identity/worth, 181; resentment of, 21, 63; reversal of,

225

cosmopolitanism (*continued*)
24; supposed dogmatism of, 139; as threat, 25, 37, 44

Coulter, Ann, 96, 174, 176

creationism, 120

criticism, 15–17, 56, 73, 104, 178–79

Darwin, Charles, 77, 111

democracy: bigotry in relation to, 13–14, 112; bigotry persistent in, 160; capitalist, 185–86; elitist opposition to, 133; elitists' response to, 130; identity and subjectivity in, 52–53; and religion, 124; status of individuals in, 36–37; subalterns and, 52–53

Democratic Party, 162, 166, 170, 172, 176, 192

demonization, 61, 89

deracination, 35, 43, 93

Dewey, John, 20

Dixiecrats, 162, 166

Dostoevsky, Fyodor, 117

double standards, 5, 7, 33, 64–67, 163, 184

Douglass, Frederick, 48

Dreyfus, Alfred, 43

Drumont, Édouard, 43

Du Bois, W. E. B., 138

Eco, Umberto, vii, 28

economy and economics: bankers blamed for crises in, 72; collapse of (2008), 163, 169; downturns in Middle Eastern, 79; "household" perspective on, 146–47, 170; ignorance of, 165; libertarian view of, 164. *See also* capitalism

Eichmann, Adolf, 89

Elias, Norbert, 25

Eliot, T. S., 137

elitists, bigots as, 5–6, 126–41; alienation of, 137; and argumentation, 132, 135, 137–39; bigoted forms of, 102–3; change opposed by, 132, 134–36; conservatism of, 127, 132, 137; control sought by, 130; cynicism of, 131; enemies of, 111; exclusiveness of, 132–33; feelings of belonging among, 131; and the masses, 130, 131, 133; as natural aristocracy, 128–29; and the Other, 126–27, 129; positive aspects of, 101; prejudices of, 138–39; reactionary thought and behavior of, 132–38; and stereotypes, 138; superiority of, 126–41; in Tea Party, 168; thoughts and opinions of, 100, 110–11; types of, 126; and violence, 140

Engels, Frederick, 19, 189

English Defense League, 91

Enlightenment, 14, 40–43, 145, 215n44

establishmentarian conservatism, 132, 157, 160, 164

establishmentarian liberalism, 40

evangelists, 116–17, 213n22

evidence, 16, 28, 44, 62–63, 70–71, 73, 135; conspiracy fetishism and,

70–71, 73; disregard for, 28, 44,
   135; selective use of, 16, 62–63, 135
evil, 6, 55, 56, 67, 68, 70, 71, 87, 119,
   163

falsifiability, 35, 55, 75
family, 17–18, 55, 102–3, 143
fanaticism, 5–6, 67, 86–98, 174,
   210n31
Fanon, Frantz, 40
fascism, 19, 39, 44, 130–31
fate, 37, 54, 55, 56, 90. *See also*
   predestination
Federal Bureau of Investigation
   (FBI), 209n29
feminism, 48, 93
First Zionist Congress, 79
Ford, Richard Thompson, 190
Forrest, Nathan Bedford, 149–50
Foucault, Michel, 41
Founding Fathers, 183
Fox News, 2, 155, 177
France, 43–44, 215n43
freedom, 33, 37–38, 65, 165
freedom of speech, 35–37
Freedom-Works, 167
Freud, Sigmund, 102, 110, 148,
   211n5
Fromm, Erich, 107
fundamentalism, 2, 19, 29, 116

Gandhi, Mahatma, 51, 66–67, 125
Gates of Vienna (web site), 91–92, 96
gays and homosexuality, 3, 32, 34,
   40–41, 47, 62, 159, 185

Geller, Pamela, 61, 96
gender, Tea Party and, 169, 171, 172,
   176, 177
gender roles, 34
Genet, Jean, 40
genetics, 16, 202n3
genocide, 15, 64–65, 88, 96, 116, 118,
   158
Germany, 158, 215n43, 215n46
Gershwin, George, 149
Giffords, Gabrielle, 174
God: events determined by, 9, 55, 56,
   108; as justification for status quo,
   23; mythological thinking and, 56;
   true believers' relationship with,
   99–100, 141
Goethe, Johann Wolfgang von, vii,
   42, 119
Goldstein, Baruch, 96
government: and conspiracy, 72;
   involvement/encroachment of,
   163–65, 169, 172, 186; size and
   reach of, 170, 175, 177
Grand Mosque, Mecca, 29
Greek Orthodox Church, 79
Griffith, D. W., *Birth of a Nation*,
   61, 133
Ground Zero, New York City, 34
gun ownership, 174

Haggard, Ted, 116
Hamas, 75
Harris-Perry, Melissa, 52
hate crimes, 87, 185
hate speech, 36, 158

Hegel, Chuck, 170

Heidegger, Martin, 151

heritage, 141, 150, 153

Herr, Lucien, 43

Himmler, Heinrich, 95

Hinduism, 25, 31, 117

history: conspiracies and, 71–72; refashioning of, 9–10, 31, 150–51; revisionist, 152; withdrawal from, 55, 107–8. *See also* nostalgia

Hitler, Adolf, 16, 28, 65, 90–92, 95, 96, 118, 130, 153, 166

Hofstadter, Richard, 71

Holocaust, 66, 84, 114

homosexuality. *See* gays and homosexuality

Horkheimer, Max, 122

Huckabee, Mike, 114

human rights, 25, 162

Huntington, Samuel, 142

hysteria, 23, 68, 72, 86, 97, 108, 128

identity and subjectivity, 37–53; affirmation of, 28; community as source of, 44–46; critical perspective on, 51–52; defined by the Other, 97, 105; democracy and, 52–53; essentialism and, 104; and exclusion, 47; fluidity of, 30; freedom and, 37–38; group influence on, 107; of the Other, 27–28, 52; and power, 105; reactionary notion of, 42–43; roles as constitutive of, 105–9; stereotypes and, 104; stunted form of, 104; of subalterns, 27, 47–49; and submission to authority, 103; variability of, 11. *See also* self-worth

identity deficit, 10–11, 22, 30, 63–64, 161, 180, 202n7

identity politics, 41–42, 47–50, 191, 193

imaginings, bigots': about community, 46; about events and occurrences, 9; about their world, 5; about the Other, 27, 28, 86–87; about the past, 145–46; in chaotic world, 109

immigrants, 3, 17, 32, 111–12, 158–59

imperialism, 31, 140. *See also* colonialism

income and wealth distribution, 18, 163, 168, 171, 177, 186, 187, 190, 192, 220n30

intellectuals, 1, 8, 21, 24, 31, 43, 68, 139

intelligent design, 111, 120

interest groups, 47–48

Internet, 29

intolerance, 2–3, 34, 36–37, 82, 99, 115–16, 118–19, 163–64, 173, 178. *See also* tolerance

intuition, 43, 44, 101

Islam, 33–34, 69–70, 91–93, 117, 125. *See also* Muslims

Israel, 31, 33, 40, 46, 61, 70, 79, 82–85, 95, 158, 209n24

Jacobi, Friedrich, 116

Jaurès, Jean, 43

Index

Jefferson, Thomas, 124, 128
Jews, 3; authentic, 38; bigotry of, 50;
    characteristics of, 32; Christian
    embrace of, 33; conspiracy theories
    about, 74–85; conspiracy theories
    held by, 82–84; double standard
    applied by, 65, 66; and modernity,
    144; Nazism and, 26; and Obama,
    69; Orthodox, 65; as Other, 27–28;
    slaughters perpetrated by, 117;
    stereotypes of, 61; suffering decried
    by, 25; as threat, 17. *See also*
    anti-Semitism
John Birch Society, 166
Johnson, Samuel, 131

Kafka, Franz, 39
Kant, Immanuel, 24, 121, 182, 215n44
King, Martin Luther, Jr., 51, 125, 161
knowledge: fixity of, 110; intuitive,
    44; lack or refusal of, 7, 27, 30–31,
    63, 67, 138–39; mythological
    thinking as basis for, 56–57; of
    others and oneself, 181–82;
    selective use of, 63; of true
    believers, 116
Know-Nothing Party, 166
Koch brothers, 167
Kristol, Irving, 139
Ku Klux Klan, 11, 19, 26, 50–51, 61,
    106, 149, 150, 166, 209n29

LaHaye, Beverly, 204n16
language, 8, 34–35, 56, 58, 82, 101,
    157, 173–74

Latinos, 47, 50, 152, 186
Lee, Spike, 48–49, 143
Le Pen, Marine, 159
Levinas, Emmanuel, 33
Lewis, Sinclair: *Elmer Gantry*,
    213n22; *Main Street*, 148
Lewontin, Richard, 202n3
liberalism: bigotry in, 19–20, 159; of
    the bourgeoisie, 19; capitalism and,
    18; chauvinist version of, 147;
    cosmopolitanism and, 182; and
    criticism, 16; elitist opposition to,
    135–36; establishmentarian, 40;
    fanaticism and, 210n31; inadequacy
    of, 40–42; pluralism and, 10; and
    religion, 115–16, 123–26; and rule
    of law, 14, 35, 161, 180, 182; so-
    cialism linked to, 20, 161; stereo-
    types about, 176–77; subaltern
    embrace of, 24; supposed dogma-
    tism of, 139; as term of opprobrium,
    1; true believers vs., 115–16, 118
libertarianism, 164, 168–69
Limbaugh, Rush, 2
Lueger, Karl, 58
Luger, Richard, 170

Macdonald, Andrew. *See* Pierce,
    William Luther, *The Turner Diaries*
Maistre, Joseph de, 41–42
Malik, Kenan, 15
"mammies," 149
Mandela, Nelson, 51
Manicheanism. *See* binary
    oppositions

229

Mann, Thomas, 117
Marcuse, Herbert, 100
marriage, 3, 204n16
Martin, Trayvon, 191
Marx, Karl, 13, 19, 69–70, 77, 121–22
masculinity, 93
mass media, 29
Maurras, Charles, 43
McCain, John, 175
McCarthy, Joseph, 166
McConnell, Mitch, 1
McPherson, Aimee Semple, 116
McQueen, Butterfly, 149
Memmi, Albert, 205n23
Mendelssohn, Moses, 125
Merah, Mohammed, 86
Middle East, 79–84, 88
military, gays in, 62
Mills, C. W., 183–84
modernity, 13–53; bigotry elicited by
    principles and effects of, 14–15,
    23–25, 29, 63, 111, 167; bigotry's
    uses of, 15–16; capitalism and,
    14, 17–20; confusion caused by,
    113–14; cosmopolitanism and, 25,
    44, 106, 168; identity deficit arising
    from, 63–64; Jews and, 144; myths
    vs., 55; and religion, 120–24;
    resentment of, 21–22, 120; roots
    of, 14; true believers and, 113–14,
    120–21
Montesquieu, Baron de, 183
morality, of bigots, 67, 153
moral majority, 166
Morris, Dick, 176

multiculturalism, 1, 30, 63, 106, 152,
    159
Muslim Brotherhood, 70
Muslims, 3, 31, 64, 66, 119. *See also*
    Arabs; Islam
Mussolini, Benito, 16
mythological thinking, 54–98;
    characteristics of, 54; conspiracy
    fetishism and, 68–86; cosmological
    and existential character of, 54–57;
    double standards employed in,
    64–67; fanaticism and, 86–98;
    justificatory use of, 55–56; moder-
    nity vs., 55; stereotypes and, 58–64

NAACP, 150
narcissism, 110, 148
nationalism, 42–45, 84, 146
Nation of Islam, 75
Native Americans, 152
natural aristocracy, 128–29
nature: events determined by, 56; as
    fixed, 24, 51; as justification for
    status quo, 23; order of, 9, 17–18,
    34, 61, 128
Nazism, 11, 15, 26, 39, 66, 106, 136,
    143, 172
neoconservatism, 128, 139, 162–63
Neo-Nazism, 75, 106
neurosis, 22–23. *See also* objective
    neurosis
Niebuhr, Reinhold, 119
Nietzsche, Friedrich, 22, 77, 204n13
9/11 terrorist attacks, 9, 75, 88, 137,
    163

Index

nostalgia, 30, 106, 141, 144–46, 151, 178

Nuremburg Trials, 39

Obama, Barack, 1–2, 69, 82, 163, 169, 173, 174, 176, 177, 191

objective neurosis, 22, 111

Occupied Territories, 31, 46, 83

open society, 9, 16

Opus Dei, 125

O'Reilly, Bill, 176, 177

organicism, 5, 41, 42, 44, 100, 144, 146, 148, 151

Orientalism, 163, 217n9

originalism, 183–85

the Other, 26–37; absence/denial/ erasure of, 141–43, 145, 147, 184–85; attitudes toward, 31–32, 95, 126–27; bigot's identity/self defined by, 97, 105; characteristics of, 6, 8; constraints on, 183; construction of, 27; cosmopolitanism and, 181–82; elitists and, 129; fanaticism toward, 86–87; fear of, 32, 125; gaining knowledge and experience of, 151, 181–82; identity/subjectivity of, 27–28, 52; inferiority of, 6, 8, 126, 129, 140; sameness and lack of distinctiveness of, 26, 28, 57–58, 88–89, 97; Tea Party and, 171–72; as threat, 61–62. *See also* subalterns

Palestinians, 40, 46, 50, 82–83, 85, 158

Palin, Sarah, 171, 174, 175

paranoia, 24, 31–32, 67, 68, 72, 77, 80, 83, 86, 89, 97–98, 110, 164, 178

Parens, Henri, 31

parochialism, 7, 10, 17, 21, 41, 51, 115, 129, 145, 211n3

Penn, William, 125

persecution, feelings of, 9, 22–23, 98, 168

personal experience: bigots' world view based on, 43–45; grandiose conceptions of, 94; identity arising from, 43–44, 51; justificatory use of, 51, 62–63; parochialism fostered by reliance on, 41; stereotypes justified by, 62–63; of subalterns, 40–41

pessimism, 23, 73, 92, 108, 113, 168

Pierce, William Luther, *The Turner Diaries*, 89–92, 96

Piven, Frances Fox, 52, 69

Plessner, Helmuth, 46

pluralism, 10, 15, 36–37, 112, 125, 152

Podhoretz, Norman, 162

politics: bigotry in, 159–63, 179; public participation in, 130, 132–33; religion and, 124; symbolism in, 190; tactics in, 11–12; Tea Party and, 167–78; in United States, 166; violence and, 88. *See also* democracy; identity politics

Pollack, Friedrich, 132

Poor Peoples' Campaign, 47, 192

populism, 6, 11, 126, 127, 145, 168

Powell, Colin, 169
predestination, 59, 60, 129. *See also* fate
prejudice: adaptation of, 32–33; appeal of, 7; clustering of, 26; denial or ignoring of, 157; of the elite, 129; elitists and, 138–39; etymology of, 7; forms of, 24; imprisoning nature of, 5, 63; knowledge in relation to, 138–39; of marginal groups, 21; normality of, 5, 14; prereflective character of, 102, 105; reason vs., 43; reinforcement of, 108; science vs., 16; stereotypes and, 58. *See also* stereotypes
Press TV, 70
privilege, 5, 9, 22, 23, 30, 33, 48, 110, 136, 151, 162
projection, 22, 32, 68, 71, 72, 80, 86–87, 95, 105, 128, 152
Protocols of the Elders of Zion, 74–81, 85

race: chauvinism and, 144; class in relation to, 192; Confederate nostalgia and, 150; fanatical thinking about, 90–92, 97; income by, 186; life chances influenced by, 186–87; stereotypes and, 62; in the United States, 144; U.S. Supreme Court and, 220n26
Rahimi, Mohammad-Reza, 75
rationality. *See* thinking and rationality

reactionary thought and behavior, 8, 25, 41–42, 132–38, 145, 160, 163, 166–67, 170, 178
reciprocity, 10, 42, 51, 142, 180
relativism, 10, 152
religion: authoritarian, 103; bigotry within, 47; blame assigned for supposed breaches of, 114; changes in, 29–30, 155; conservatism in, 164; double standard applied in, 65; foundational role of, 21; and gay marriage/rights opposition, 3, 47; intolerance concerning, 115–16, 118–19, 163–64; liberalism and, 115–16, 123–26; Marx on, 121–22; mitigation of suffering as characteristic of, 25; modernity and, 120–24; mythological thinking and, 55; politics and, 124; privacy of, 124–26; reason in relation to, 121–24; slaughter justified by, 117–18; true believers and, 115–19 124–25; varieties of, 114–16, 124. *See also* fundamentalism
repressive tolerance, 36–37
Republican Party, 162, 164, 169–71, 172–78
resentment, 5, 17, 21, 23, 31–32, 63, 99, 120, 152, 168, 204n13
responsibility: ethical, 38–39; imputed to adversaries, 32; lack or refusal of, 7, 10, 35, 54–55, 96; personal, 38–39, 54, 157, 187; of the powerless, 47
rights, 25, 124, 162, 174, 180:

right-wing movements, 1, 20, 166, 170

Robertson, Pat, 114

Roe v. Wade, 184

roles of the bigot, 5–6, 8, 99–153; anxiety a product of, 110–11; the chauvinist, 141–53; the elitist, 126–41; function of, 6, 99–100, 105, 154; identity/subjectivity and, 105–9; positive aspects of, 101; rationales of, 99–100; and relationship to authority, 102–4, 110; the true believers, 113–26

Roma, 159

Romero, Óscar, 125

Romney, Mitt, 174–76, 189

Rosenberg, Alfred, 153

Rosenzweig, Franz, 45

Rove, Karl, 176

Rubin, Jennifer, 82–83

rule of law, 14, 35, 161, 180, 182, 186

Said, Edward, 85, 217n9

Salafis, 125

Sandy Hook Elementary School, Newtown, Connecticut, 70, 114

Santorum, Rick, 171

Sartre, Jean-Paul, 4, 22, 37–40, 99, 108–9, 131, 181

Saudi Arabia, 95, 158, 163

Savage, Michael, 2

savior fantasies, 20, 71, 87, 94

Scalia, Antonin, 184

scapegoats, 55–56, 148, 158

Scheler, Max, 22

Schlesinger, Arthur, 166

Schoenberg, Arnold, 58

science, 15–16, 21, 63, 111, 120, 164

Scripture, 117–19, 123, 183

secularism, 15, 21, 111, 114, 122, 189

self. *See* identity and subjectivity

self-referentiality, 45, 57, 94, 101, 105

self-worth, 5, 22, 103, 120

Selma, Alabama, 149–50

Sharia law, 54–55, 70

slavery, 31, 150

Snowe, Olympia, 170

social character, 105–7

socialism, 1, 17, 19–20, 24, 158, 161

social justice, 112, 162, 187

social movements, 187–88, 193

society, 20, 35, 92. *See also* civilization

solidarity: among bigots, 45, 50–51; cosmopolitanism and, 182; within interest groups, 48; with the Other, 66–67; among subalterns, 18–19, 40, 41, 51, 191–94

the South, 149–50, 162, 173

Stein, Gertrude, 137

stereotypes: concept of, 58; as constraints, 59–61; elitists and, 138; enemies delineated by, 57–58; and identity, 104; interests underlying formation or use of, 58; justificatory use of, 5, 7, 56, 60–62; of liberals, 176–77; mythological thinking and, 7, 55, 58–64; negative, 59–64;

stereotypes (*continued*)
neutral, 59; origins of, 63; of the Other, 27, 31; persistence of, 164; prejudice and, 58; prereflective character of, 7, 31, 57; selective thinking underlying, 62; of the stranger, 148; transfer of, 62. *See also* prejudice
stranger anxiety, 31–32, 158
strangers, 61, 146, 148–49
strict constructionism, 183–85
structural societal factors, 71, 128, 165, 187
subalterns: attitudes of, 31; attitudes toward, 5, 8, 9–10, 31; bigotry of, 46–47, 49–50, 66; characteristics of, 6, 8; conflicts among, 46–50, 191; and democracy, 52–53; dependence of bigots/oppressors on, 205n23; differences among, 181; identity/ subjectivity of, 27, 47–50; inferiority of, 23, 27, 56, 67, 128, 133; irremediability of, 127–28, 132–35; moral shortcomings of, 127; principles and politics of, 24; public participation blocked for, 130, 132–33; resistance by, 39–40; solidarity among, 18–19, 40, 41, 51, 191–94; status of, 23, 29; sufferings of, 9–10; threat posed by, 27; violence against, 174; violence imputed to, 140. *See also* the Other
subjectivity. *See* identity and subjectivity

Sunday, Billy, 116
superiority, feelings of, 5, 6, 10, 20, 23, 24, 28, 32, 35, 55, 56, 103, 113, 126–41, 145
Supreme Court, U.S., 220n26
Swaggart, Jimmy, 116
"Swanee" (song), 149

Tea Party, 12, 106, 163, 164, 167–78, 171; birth of, 169; funding of, 167; and gender, 169, 171, 172, 176, 177; ideology of, 168–69, 172; influence of, 170–71, 174–78; membership of, 167–68; and the Other, 171–73; political platform of or influenced by, 173, 175; and presidential election, 175–76; violence associated with, 174
television sit-coms, 147
terrorism, 88, 90–91, 96. *See also* 9/11 terrorist attacks
thinking and rationality: intuition vs., 43; mythological thinking vs., 54, 56; religion in relation to, 121–24; roles as influence on, 99–100; simplicity of bigot's, 7. *See also* circular reasoning; knowledge; mythological thinking; reactionary thought and behavior
tolerance, 10, 35–37, 181. *See also* intolerance
tradition: chauvinism and, 142, 153; critical perspective on, 52; events determined by, 108; as justification

for status quo, 7, 23, 30; mythological thinking grounded in, 55, 56; the Other as constructed by, 97; preservation of, 9, 10
transgender people, 3, 40, 159
Treitschke, Heinrich von, 138
true believers, 5–6, 65, 113–26; bigoted forms of, 102–3; blaming of victims by, 114; enemies of, 111; and fundamentalism, 116; intolerance of, 115; liberalism as enemy of, 115–16, 118; and modernity, 113–14, 120–21; positive aspects of, 101; relationship of, to God, 113–26; religious life of, 115–19, 124–25; slaughters perpetrated by, 117–18; in Tea Party, 168; thoughts and opinions of, 99–100, 110–11, 119–21; and totalitarianism, 117
truth, 10, 44, 56, 99–100, 116, 118–19. *See also* falsifiability
The Turner Diaries (Pierce), 89–92, 96

United Nations, 2, 69, 173
United States: bigotry in, 166–67; chauvinism in, 143–44; income and wealth distribution in, 186, 187, 220n30; social justice in, 187
universalism, 10, 14, 16, 40–43, 49
Uris, Leon, *Exodus*, 83, 209n24
U.S. Constitution, 183–85
U.S. Supreme Court, 220n26
us vs. them mentality, 24, 28, 33, 57–58, 73, 84, 163

victims: bigots as, 23, 70, 95, 97; blaming of, 22–23, 32, 114, 151; conflicts among, 46–47; internalization of bigotry by, 46–47
Vietnam War, 40, 144
violence, 13, 87–89, 111, 140, 153, 174, 209n28
Voltaire, 124
Voting Rights Act (1965), 135, 162, 173, 184

Wagner, Richard, 137
Waters, Ethel, 149
Weber, Max, 15, 58
welfare and the welfare state, 11, 17, 20, 32, 69, 128, 135, 142, 146, 155, 157, 161–65, 169, 170, 189–90
West, Allen, 172
West, Cornel, 16
West Side Story (film), 46–47
Wilders, Geert, 159
Williams, Roger, 125
Wittgenstein, Ludwig, 102
women: characteristics of, 32; chauvinist view of, 143; public issues centered on, 184–85; status of, 40; stereotypes of, 59–60; Tea Party view of, 171; as threat, 93
workers and working class, 17, 19
World War II, 38–39

Yousafzai, Malala, 73

Zola, Émile, 43